Battlegrou[]

VILLERS-[]
and the Five Ridges

With the continued expansion of the Battleground series a **Battleground Europe Club** has been formed to benefit the reader. The purpose of the Club is to keep members informed of new titles and key developments by way of a quarterly newsletter, and to offer many other reader-benefits. Membership is free and by registering an interest you can help us predict print runs and thus maintain prices at their present levels. Please call the office 01226 734555, or send your name and address along with a request for more information to:
Battleground Europe Club
Pen & Sword Books Ltd, 47 Church Street, Barnsley, South Yorkshire S70 2AS

Battleground Europe

VILLERS-PLOUICH
and the Five Ridges

K.W. Mitchinson

Series editor
Nigel Cave

LEO COOPER

First published in 1999 by
LEO COOPER
an imprint of
Pen & Sword Books Limited
47 Church Street, Barnsley, South Yorkshire S70 2AS

Copyright © K W Mitchinson

ISBN 0 85052 658 2

A CIP catalogue of this book is available
from the British Library

Printed by Redwood Books Limited
Trowbridge, Wiltshire

*For up-to-date information on other titles produced under the Leo Cooper imprint,
please telephone or write to:*

Pen & Sword Books Ltd, FREEPOST, 47 Church Street
Barnsley, South Yorkshire S70 2AS
Telephone 01226 734222

CONTENTS

INTRODUCTION BY SERIES EDITOR

The area around Villers-Plouich was heavily contested over in both 1917 and in 1918. Ground nearby was fought over as part of the right hook of the Battle of Cambrai in November 1917 and it saw some of the very bitterest fighting in the approach to the Canal du Nord in September 1918. Much of the action here – and indeed the time spent in holding the line – was characterised by grim determination in a part of the world that is even more devoid of topographical features than elsewhere on the old British front.

What makes it a delightful part of northern France for the battlefield visitor is that it remains so relatively unspoilt, allowances having been made for the autoroute that carves through the eastern edge of the area covered by the book. It is easy to follow the route by use of the trench maps, as so many of the roads and tracks have remained in the same

(or almost the same) locations. Because of the lack of many large villages, and because the woods and copses have often been allowed to grow back, it is possible to get a feel for what it must have been like, at least to look at, in the spring of 1917 when the British first came here. Of course this rural idyll was soon shattered by the sound of warfare and the ground by the pounding of thousands upon thousands of shells and mortars. The contrast in this respect is stark: then a hive of activity, albeit often carried out as inconspicuously as possible; now an unhurried and tranquil atmosphere dominates.

This is another part of the old Western Front that is

all too often missed off the schedule. Yet it deserves to be examined far more closely by those of us who come afterwards. This is where the later lessons of the war were learnt, and where victory was won. The years 1917 and 1918 need to be taken far more seriously by more of us if the image of the First World War is ever to move away from the summer of 1916. There remains plenty of evidence of military activity in this part of the world whether it be the trench outlines in Gauche Wood or one of the numerous concrete fortifications erected by the German engineers, part of the Hindenburg Line. And of course there are the cemeteries; it is one of the benefits of books such as this that a story can now be added to the rows of individuals and unknowns that are to be found in these English gardens in the fields that surround Villers-Plouich.

Nigel Cave, Ely Place, London

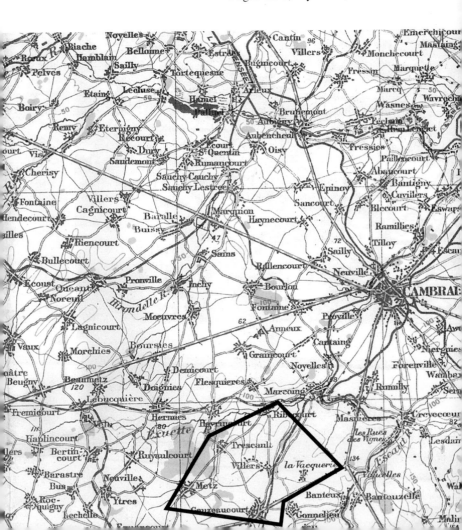

INTRODUCTION

The village of Villers-Plouich is largely unknown or unrecognised by most British visitors to the Western Front. Away from the more usual stomping grounds of the Somme and Ypres, the village and its surrounding countryside rarely witness the passage of British cars or walkers. Those few who do venture along its roads and tracks generally know little of the battles and engagements fought eighty years ago over its rolling fields and among the now smart cottages.

In the cold, miserable Spring of 1917 Fourth Army pursued the Kaiser's forces across a largely devastated swathe of land. The Germans were in the process of staging a planned withdrawal towards the shelter of the almost completed Hindenburg Line. The position of this supposedly impregnable defensive system had been chosen with care and the construction executed with a thoroughness which had long typified the actions of the German army. As the retreat neared the Hindenburg Line, German resistance stiffened. Certain villages to its west had been designated areas where the final rearguard actions would inflict as much damage, casualties and delay upon the pursuing forces as possible. Among these villages were Metz, Gouzeaucourt, Beaucamp, La Vacquerie and Villers-Plouich. Several of these small clusters of farm cottages lay in valleys while others sat atop the rises of the undulating land. These ridges were soon christened by the troops who eventually captured them: Fusilier, Borderer, Welsh and Highland

Heading north on the D917 one mile south of Fins. The dark mass of trees in the centre is Dessart Wood. Fins and the wood were taken by 2/RB on 30 March 1917.

Two German prisoners, complete with machine guns, escorted by a soldier of the 51st Division near Trescault, 20 November 1917. (IWM Q6274)

Ridges bore the names of regiments of the 40th Division who fought for their slopes and crests. Once these ridges fell, British units were in close proximity to the outpost line of the main German system. Any further advance would necessitate a major and costly offensive against the wire, pill boxes and trenches of the Hindenburg Line itself.

As British efforts to break the deadlock of the Western Front in 1917 were concentrated further north, the Villers-Plouich sector became in many ways the epitome of trench warfare: an extensive system of generally well constructed fire, support and reserve trenches, reasonably comfortable areas to the rear for training and resting troops out of the line, regular early morning and evening exchanges by the artillery, almost constant nocturnal patrolling of No Man's Land, frequent raids upon enemy sapheads and outpost positions and a steady, if undramatic, increase in the number of soldiers' cemeteries.

The area exploded into a period of sustained and awesome violence during the Cambrai offensive in late 1917. It witnessed then the initial fruits of a largely unexpected victory, to be followed only days later by the bitterness of defeat. Ten months later it again had armies fighting within its folds and ruins. On this occasion, prolonged and bloody conflict, all of which was an integral part of a far broader scheme, finally expelled the invader from the ridges and villages. While never perhaps one of the most pivotal of areas, the recapture of Highland, Beaucamp and Welsh Ridges by IV Corps in September 1918 was an essential contribution to the eventual, greater victory.

The line of trees marks Flag Ravine east of the railway on the D56. The steeple of Gonnelieu church pokes above Fusilier Ridge.

ACKNOWLEDGMENTS

The information within these pages has been gathered from a variety of primary and secondary written evidence and from many years of walking and cycling the area. Detail from unit war diaries has been supplemented by divisional, regimental and battalion histories. As the present volume is not intended as an academic work, I have followed the same practice as in its two companion volumes on Epéhy and Riqueval by referencing only direct quotations. The bibliography notes the secondary sources consulted but to save space the several dozen war diaries and their PRO index numbers have not been listed.

Several individuals and institutions have helped with the writing and production of this book. In particular I extend my thanks to the Trustees of the Public Record Office and the Imperial War Museum for permission to use written and photographic material from their collections. As always, Mary Bayliss and Phillip Powell at the IWM's Department of Printed Books willingly offered their time, initiative and expertise; the ladies of Accrington Library were again generous with their help and facilities. At Barnsley the seemingly indefatigable Barbara and the unnervingly tranquil Roni have eased through the production in their usual professional manner. My thanks to Nigel Cave, Kevin Kelly, David Key and Paul McCue who, each in their own particular field, have provided knowledgeable and essential information. Thanks also to the numerous French farmers who tolerate my presence in the most unlikely places and who invariably attempt to answer my frequently incomprehensible questions.

Finally, my special appreciation to JB for the many happy hours spent walking the ridges in often the foulest of weather.

NOTE:

Spelling of regimental names are as found in the Official History.

There were often inconsistencies in the way British cartographers noted and spelt village and feature names. For example Good Man Farm is sometimes marked as Good Old Man Farm, a more literal translation of the farm's French name. Similarly, there remains confusion over the way some village names are spelt today. The Michelin has Beaucamp while the IGN has Beaucamps.

GENERAL ADVICE

The advice given in the other books of the series applies equally well here. Most British visitors take the Michelin 1:200000 No.53 when visiting the Somme; this map covers the Villers-Plouich area. For more detailed coverage, the IGN Blue and Green Series are useful. Number 2707E of the Blue Series includes the area covered by this book. They can be bought in decent bookshops in the UK and are readily available in towns such as Albert and Bapaume. However, to acquire a thorough and intimate appreciation of the land, trench maps are indispensible. The 1:10,000 sheets are available from the IWM's Department of Printed Books and the Western Front Association. The relevant sheets are 57C SE 1, 2, 3 & 4 and 57C NE 3 & 4.

If you are driving down from the north on the A26-E17, come off at

A German photo of Fins chateau before it was shattered by gunfire and explosive charges in March 1917. The bust remains today on the village green, close to the war memorial. (IWM Q45455)

Buried beneath the railway south of Marcoing this German bunker lies on the west side of the track, 60m north of where it passes beneath the motorway.

Exit 9. This is immediately after La Vacquerie rest area (no services). The D917 then takes you into the heart of the area. If travelling from the west, and if time is of the essence, take the D917 out of Péronne as far as Fins and then revert to minor roads. A slightly longer but perhaps more appropriate route, would go through Combles, Bouchavesnes and Moislains. The crest of the D149 east of Bouchavesnes crosses the area of Pallas and Fritz Trenches. Several routes will be found at the back of the book and it is suggested that a preliminary tour of the area will help the visitor to appreciate the general lie of the land and the relative positions of the villages.

Accommodation in the area is very limited. There are several hotels in Péronne and Cambrai, but as most British visitors will probably be staying near Arras or Albert and Villers-Plouich is only 40 minutes drive from each, stay at your usual lodgings. Before you leave, do some shopping and fill up with petrol or diesel. Gouzeaucourt does possess some shops, a café and a PTT but they tend to close for two hours at lunchtime. Better to have your liquid and solid sustenance with you when you set off.

In addition to your supplies, take a waterproof, boots, compass, field glasses, hat and sun cream. The weather on the ridges can be ferocious: howling winds, sleet and snow in winter and a blazing, unrelenting sun in summer. Unlike the Somme, shelter or cover is not so easily found. Use your common sense when walking among the villages and on the higher ground. The suggested routes stick to farm tracks and lanes and so should you. The farmers are friendly and cooperative but they do not appreciate cars on lanes obstructing their tractors and people wandering over their sown fields. The best time to visit the Western Front is late autumn or early spring; with the crops gone or not yet sprung, the folds and contours of the land are so much easier to appreciate.

Take your usual measures with regard to medical insurance, or at least make sure you carry a E111 and that your tetanus jabs are up to date. You might also be required to show a green card for motor insurance, a spare set of bulbs, a warning triangle and a first aid kit. On the spot fines from a bored gendarme tend to spoil an otherwise enjoyable day. If cycling, take the normal spare inner tube, spanners and levers.

Finally, go to the area with an open mind. There are not many physical remains to see and for various reasons it has not acquired the emotive appeal of the Somme. What it does offer however, is some beautiful scenery, a great deal of space, tranquillity and fields steeped in history.

The low lying marshes of the Somme presented tremendous difficulties to the British troops pursuing the retreating Germans in March 1917. This pontoon was constructed near Péronne.

Chapter One

INTO THE WILDERNESS

At the beginning of 1917 British and Dominion forces remained locked in the unresolved battle of attrition on the Somme. Among the once fertile fields and comely villages, the warring armies killed and maimed each other on a scale unparalleled in history. Six months of unrelenting slaughter had brought an advance of roughly six miles of desolate land. Countering this somewhat dubious achievement, the casualty list on both sides had spiralled beyond imagination and the morale of the opposing armies had sunk to a low, but nevertheless resolute, depth. Among the water-filled shell holes and shattered trenches which scattered or snaked themselves across the downs and valleys of the tortured land, the Empire's conscript and volunteer armies battled it out with their equally determined foe. A howling wind brought drenching sleet and numbing snow to seek out the holes and crevices in which men huddled for shelter. It penetrated their leaden clothing, chilled their aching, burdened bones and added to the misery inflicted by their enemy. To the freezing troops of Fourth and Fifth Armies, the new year heralded little prospect of earthly salvation.

Short respites from the line might bring a change of clothes, a few beers in a smoky estaminet and even a 'bed' which did not consist of a mixture of mud, water and enemy shells. At the end of the all too short pause, they knew they would return to the same or similar stretch of

The deliberate destruction of roadside trees was a ploy used by the Germans to delay the British pursuit. Taylor Library

British officers studying maps during the German withdrawal. The destruction of landmarks was another tactic employed to hinder the advancing Allies. Taylor Library

sodden land and be expected to raise their weary bodies from the ineluctable mud and assault the equally broken positions held by the enemy. The patriotism and enthusiasm with which men flocked to enlist in the heady days of 1914 were long since spent. True, some young idealists remained, but they were in the minority. A majority of the 1914 men were by now either dead, permanently maimed or in safer jobs with training battalions. Most of those who manned the front positions and the gun batteries behind them were there because they had been conscripted or because they had not been lucky enough to receive a decent blighty. Yet, despite the weather, the seemingly endless routine of death, exhaustion and unchanging food, the morale of the British armies did not break. A stolid determination to see the job through replaced the earlier enthusiasm, but there remained a pride in their amateurish professionalism and a stoicism which would see the armies survive the depredations of winter and provide the springboard for a new offensive.

On the other side of the often poorly defined No Man's Land, the German armies faced similar problems. The Somme had exacted a huge toll of Germany's finest troops and to the survivors the prospect of victory remained as distant as it did to their British counterparts. The British blockade was biting deep into the supplies required not only by the army but also to their families at home. Furthermore, despite some massive German victories in the east, the Russian army had still not cracked. The fall in morale and the expensive demands of a war on two fronts caused unease at German High Command. The increasing concern was about to result in the invocation of contingency plans.

After only three months of the Somme campaign the German authorities had ordered construction to begin of a major new defensive line miles to the east of where the fighting was currently taking place. This new system, which the Germans called the Siegfried Stellung but which the British soon referred to as the Hindenburg Line, remained shrouded in mystery during the poor weather of the winter months.

A platoon of British soldiers picks its way through the ruined streets of Péronne.

Cavalry units were active during the pursuit towards the Hindenburg Line. The deep mud and fodder shortage meant that squadrons could only be used for limited periods. Taylor Library

Allied Intelligence knew the Germans were busy with forced labour in their rear areas but initially assumed that this work was merely yet another defensive system, of which there were several already complete. The Germans, though, were thinking along different lines. The Siegfried Stellung was designed not as just another series of substantial trenches and concrete pill boxes, but as a sophisticated zone of defence in depth against which the Allied armies would hurl themselves to destruction.

Although there appears to have been a wide degree of agreement within the German High Command about the advantages of constructing such a zone, there was less agreement over how it should be utilised. It was seen by some senior officers as a fall-back position in case the Somme proved to be too much of a drain on Germany's manpower and matériel. If this were to be the case, a voluntary withdrawal might then be authorised. Such a move would have the advantage of eliminating two salients, thereby saving an estimated 14 divisions. In the view of another faction, the line should be immediately occupied and so provide the army with a strong position in which it could remain until decisive political and economic factors came into play. Even a voluntary withdrawal did not, in Ludendorff's mind, necessarily prevent the German army sallying forth and delivering, when circumstances permitted, a crushing counter-attack upon the Allied armies. The outbreak of revolution in Russia, although by no means a promise of peace, was an encouraging development. Ludendorff was also prepared to wait for the second campaign of unrestricted submarine warfare to extract its toll of Allied resources and morale. If these assumptions were correct, within twelve months the fortunes of war might well have swung in Germany's favour. Until then, her forces would have to survive the anticipated Allied spring and summer offensives. In view of the manpower situation, they would be far more able to resist the onslaughts from a position of strength behind a formidable defensive line.

On 28 January 1917 Crown Prince Rupprecht decided the men of First Army had suffered enough among the marshes of the Ancre and demanded that a withdrawal to the new line be authorised. Five days later the Kaiser signed the order and the countdown of the 35 Alberich days - in which the administrative and support units would withdraw and the land be laid waste - began. From 16 March four marching days were allowed for the bulk of the fighting troops to be in positions within the zone or the villages immediately to its front. However, Rupprecht was convinced that the state of First Army necessitated an immediate withdrawal. Rather than wait until 16 March, he ordered his forces on the Ancre to begin their march eastward. On 23 February British patrols of the 18th Division (Fifth Army), discovered that German trenches near Petit Miraumont had been abandoned and that several dugouts were ablaze. Further reports also indicating a major German withdrawal soon began to arrive at Corps HQ. It became obvious that in front of Fifth Army, German forces were withdrawing across a zone which their deliberate devastation had turned into a wasteland.

The situation remained unchanged in front of Rawlinson's Fourth Army. A raid by units of the 8th Division on 27 February failed and an attack by 12/KRRC of the 20th Division the following day near Sailly-Saillisel was repulsed with substantial losses. A German prisoner taken during a counter-attack told his captors that his comrades were under orders to withdraw in the 'near future', but that for the time being they were to hold their positions. Bloody confirmation of this came on 4 March when two brigades of the 8th Division attacked Pallas and Fritz trenches near Bouchavesnes. The objective of the attack was to throw the enemy from the crests lying west of Moislains. If the heights could be secured it would give Fourth Army observation over the steep valley through which the Tortille flows between Moislains and Haut Allaines. Possession of the crest would, it was believed, make the German hold on Moislains untenable. A heavy bombardment, supplemented by artillery brigades of the nearby 40th Division, preceded the infantry assault in the murky light of a Somme day. After some hard fighting, the 2/Berkshire, 1/Worcestershire and 2/Northants eventually gained their objectives and indeed actually overran them; but at heavy cost. In the initial assault each of the three attacking battalions lost over 200 casualties and in a subsequent German counter-attack the following day sustained further substantial losses. Appreciating the importance of the position, German artillery, supported by numerous determined infantry assaults, hammered away at the newly won trenches.

Despite the success of the British attack, the Germans were not prepared to fall in unquestioningly with Rawlinson's assumptions. The enemy did withdraw in front of the 8th Division on 12 March but, opposite the 20th Division on the right, he showed no such inclination until 17 March. On that date, troops of the 40th Division south of Moislains discovered that the Germans had abandoned their front line. On 18 March XV Corps crossed the Canal du Nord east of Moislains but were held up by a strong rearguard entrenched on the Nurlu-Péronne road. As this crest-top position was known by the British to be part of a defensive line called R3, the delay was anticipated. Further strong resistance was encountered at Equancourt and Aizecourt-le-Bas. Cavalry patrols assisted with the capture of various villages and copses along the line of advance, but for several important reasons, progress was necessarily slow and deliberate. Fourth and Fifth Armies were in the process of losing certain of the divisions already earmarked for the forthcoming offensive at Arras. The loss of these divisions caused a redistribution of remaining units. On 24 March the 20th (Light) Division was transferred from XIV to XV Corps, where it joined with the 8th and 40th Divisions. The last named was then withdrawn from the line and began the arduous but essential work of improving communications across the area evacuated by the enemy. In the 8th Division, 24 Brigade was similarly withdrawn and commenced work on relaying the railway near Curlu.

Before continuing the narrative of the advance towards the Hindenburg Line, it will be worthwhile to have a quick look at the three divisions which constitute the central units of our tale.

On the outbreak of war the infantry battalions which were to form the brigades of the 8th Division were scattered throughout the Empire. They were recalled and in November 1914 the division landed at Le Havre. It fought at Neuve Chapelle, Aubers and Loos in 1915, and on the opening day of the Somme at Ovillers. As its battalions had been on several occasions reduced to handfuls, it was a regular division in name only; like most divisions on the Western Front in 1917, it was a unit filled by Derby men and conscripts.

The 20th Division, comprising 59, 60 and 61 Brigades, was a division of rifle regiments. Three battalions from each of the KRRC and the Rifle Brigade were joined by five battalions from other regiments of light infantry and the 12/King's Liverpool. The division sailed for France in July 1915. Elements of it were involved in the attack by the Meerut Division at Piètre during the following September and in the Battle of Mount Sorrel in June 1916. Having fought in Delville Wood, Guillemont, Coucelette, Morval and Le Transloy it had, like most divisions, suffered from repeated maulings on the Somme. By the early months of 1917 it was certainly a battle tested division, but retained few of its original K2 intake of 1914.

The most recent arrival of the divisions within XV Corps was the 40th. Created originally as a unit of bantam battalions, it had subsequently undergone drastic reorganisation and already had something of a chequered history. 119 Brigade had been recreated by plundering the 43rd Division of two battalions, the 1st and 2nd Glamorgan, more properly known as the 17th and 18th Welch Regiment, and the 38th Division of one battalion, the 19/RWF. The

British cyclists push their heavy machines through a ruined village in April 1917. The poor condition of the roads was a constant worry to troops and their commanders. Taylor Library

39th Division provided two non-bantam battalions for 120 Brigade, the 14/Argyll and Sutherland Highlanders and the 13/East Surrey, while the remaining two battalions, the 11/King's Own Royal Lancaster and the 14/HLI, absorbed the 12/South Lancashire and the 13/Scottish Rifles respectively in order to bring them up to strength. As it had become clear by the end of 1915 that many bantams within the battalions were not up to the physical demands of overseas service, it was decided that the division should relinquish its bantam status and become a hybrid. The third brigade, 121, retained two bantam battalions, the 13/Yorkshire (which absorbed the 18/Sherwood Foresters) and the 12/Suffolk. The remaining two units, the 20th and 21st Middlesex were removed from the 39th Division and sent to the 40th Division in February 1916. Following the Easter Rising, rumour abounded that the division was to sail for Ireland; in June 1916 the speculation proved unfounded as it left the UK for France. The division spent some months gaining trench experience in the Bully Grenay sector and then in December moved down to the Somme. For a time it constituted the right wing of the BEF.

The work performed by units of the 40th Division for the remainder of March and early April was unglamorous and, above all, fatiguing. To add to the discomfort, the weather was foul. When it was not snowing, it sleeted; if the temperature rose sufficiently to permit a thaw, the snow covered roads became flowing rivers of churned mud. The

During the German withdrawal of 1917, each corps of Third and Fourth Armies used one division to improve communications across the devastated zone. Here Pioneers are building a road across a mine crater.

deliberate German destruction of bridges and cratering of roads caused additional delays and problems. Men usually worked eight to ten hour shifts in their repair and at the end of the day sought what little comfort they could in bivvies of ground sheets erected in oceans of glutinous and soul destroying ooze.

Several battalions of the 40th Division worked under the supervision of Fourth Army Railway Construction Engineer, the individual responsible for extending the broad gauge line across the desolation to Péronne. The 12/SWB was employed in associated work involving the loading and unloading of coal and engineers' stores at Cléry. Some units were based at Linger Camp, sited among the marshes and beneath the escarpment at Curlu, while others were scattered along the length of road for which they had become responsible. The 20/Middlesex was at Moislains, the 12/Yorkshire, the divisional Pioneers, near the canal at Nurlu and the two battalions of the Welch Regiment were based at Bouchavesnes. Even the men of the 119th MGC, save for one section detached on anti-aircraft work at Etricourt, spent most of March repairing roads, and the troops of the divisional TMB were engaged in constructing horse standings for 181 Brigade, RFA. The daily grind of these fatigues was described by a diarist of the SWB as being 'very monotonous'. He further recorded that the men were 'looking forward to returning to the line'.

The conditions in which the men lived were desperate. Sappers of 231st Field Company erected Nissen huts for divisional HQ at Manancourt; less favoured troops enjoyed few such luxuries as a conventional roof and substantial walls. The 11/KORL of 120 Brigade, for example, lived among the jumbled remains of Equancourt. As the village appears not to have been built with cellars, the troops remained exposed through the dismembered roofs to the mercy of the open sky. Once they had been secured and improved by the Pioneers, officers of the 12/SWB inhabited the cellars of Etricourt; their men lived in draughty tents. The Intelligence Officer of the 13/Yorkshire seems to have relished tented accommodation, claiming that it was the 'first time' the battalion had been under canvas since its arrival in France and that it was 'quite appreciated by the men'.[1] Compared with the alternative of inadequate ground sheets suspended on short poles, tents must have seemed appealing. The Yorkshiremen were therefore perhaps a little more content than their Welsh comrades in the 18/Welch. This battalion, which according to one report refused to parade for four days in March 1915 until some particularly brutal instructors were posted elsewhere, again suffered from an excess of discipline. The men spent one day rebuilding their tented camp near Bouchavesnes in preparation for the Brigadier's inspection. On arrival the Brigadier declared the camp to be unsatisfactory and ordered that it be improved for a further inspection the following day. The troops were then marched off to work for most of a drenching night. They returned at daybreak, soaked and hungry, to strike and re-erect the camp. This additional discomfort came hard on the heels of several earlier disappointments: losing 9-0 in the brigade football cup to its sister battalion the 1st Glamorgan and 7-1 to the SWB, the release from close arrest (with the loss of 12 months' leave) of Lieutenant Whaley and the promise of a Court Martial for the absconded and recaptured Private Ramscar. Although the battalion was probably pleased to hear that the Brigadier had decided not to reinspect the camp, we can perhaps speculate on some of the prayers offered up on his behalf.

Football played a major part in what little recreation the troops were permitted. Fresh snowfalls regularly caused the postponement of matches but the final of 119 Brigade's cup was played once a thaw had begun. The pitch was punctured by numerous shell holes, the majority of which brimmed with murky, skulking water. The game, won eventually by the 12/SWB, degenerated into more of a water polo encounter.

While the men worked, usually supervised by their own officers, other more recently arrived subalterns sat through COs' lectures on tactics and training. Several of the battalions received new COs in the

British cavalry passing through the zone laid bare by shells and the enemy. French troops can be seen on the left.

period immediately before or during the German withdrawal and regularly, drafts of new subalterns reported for duty. They were all under orders to use their initiative during any pursuit and to be prepared to adapt to the changing and almost novel conditions of the now semi-open warfare. However, it was not only junior officers who were required to adapt to the developing situation.

One of the greatest concerns of senior officers of Fourth and Fifth Armies was how to keep their brigades and battalions moving in the event of a major German withdrawal. The winter weather had played havoc with the condition of the transport animals and the hock deep mud and lack of fodder meant that cavalry units could be employed for only a few days at a time. Transport officers of infantry battalions and artillery brigades regularly complained of poor animal accommodation and of their overwork. Horses which deserved a rest could rarely be afforded the luxury. In early April for instance, the transport officer of 181 Brigade, RFA (40th Division) recorded a sorry state of affairs:

Horses of the brigade are in a very low condition. During the bad weather at Marrieres Wood in December they were terribly overworked and have never had the chance to recover since. At the end of March the brigade was over 200 animals short.[2]

Over 100 horses and 36 mules were loaned to the brigade on 31 March but the unit still claimed to be over 100 animals below establishment. Furthermore, 'the continual moving is increasing the deficiency daily as a great number are not up to hard work'.[3]

Hard work and extreme powers of endurance were definitely what was expected of the units which followed the Germans across the wasteland. General Rawlinson decided that the preferred option was to pursue the enemy aggressively, but not at such a pace which might imperil the pursuers should the Germans decide to halt or counter-attack. Until the roads and railways were put into a state of good repair the infantry would be deprived of the support of heavy artillery. The anticipation was that the closer the advance drew to the Hindenburg Line, the stiffer would become the resistance. Once the line was reached, there would be no purpose in assaulting it until sufficient artillery and support services were in position. The pursuit would therefore be cautious yet determined, with lines of resistance advancing as suitable positions became available. Two weeks before the Germans actually began to withdraw on his front, Lieutenant-General Du Cane, GOC XV Corps, issued a note to his divisional commanders. It reflected his views, and certainly also those of his chief, General Rawlinson, on the tactics to be adopted when the

British cyclists fraternise with French civilians in a recently liberated village. The photo is thought to have been taken east of Péronne.

anticipated retreat should begin:

> *We must not expose large bodies of troops, unsupported by reserves, without entrenchments, and with bad communications, to the attacks of superior numbers...It is clear, then, that for a time at least we shall only be in a position to maintain touch with the retreating enemy with small forces, advanced guards or outposts. These advanced troops must of course be supported by stronger bodies, but these supporting troops will be so disposed that the outposts can fall back on them if attacked. The general idea will be to fall back if attacked and not to reinforce the front line.*[4]

Lieutenant-General Lord Cavan, GOC of nearby XIV Corps, also issued a set of instructions in preparation for the expected advance. From the experience already gained by Fifth Army, Cavan concluded that the German retreat would be 'deliberate and by carefully selected bounds'.[5] He believed that some of the difficulties encountered by Fifth Army during the pursuit were a consequence of the lack of training in open warfare and poor communication between neighbouring units. Cavan's divisional commanders were expected to organise a system in which inter-battalion, brigade and divisional links would be more efficient than those which had become apparent among Gough's units. Furthermore:

> *Initiative on the part of subordinate commanders is to be encouraged, but brigadiers and divisional commanders must keep control of the situation and allot objectives for strong patrols. Objectives once gained must be quickly and carefully consolidated...This type of fighting will afford many opportunities for outflanking hostile patrols and minor defensive positions.*[6]

Once the German retreat began, Rawlinson ordered the pursuing troops to adhere to these principles and to advance with the same deliberate care as the Germans were demonstrating in their withdrawal. These tactics were adopted for the month of March. However, at the beginning of April, Sir Douglas Haig advised Rawlinson that the French Third Army on his right planned to assault the Hindenburg Line south of St Quentin and that its commander, General Humbert, had requested that Fourth Army protect his left flank. In order to provide that close support, Rawlinson was obliged to speed up his approach to the Hindenburg Line. In front of XIV and XV Corps stood a collection of villages and copses which protected the line's outpost positions. By this time British Intelligence had a good idea of the German plans and timetable and knew that the enemy was preparing to stand and fight for these outpost villages. The time gained in delaying the British advance would provide the opportunity for troops behind the line to complete the Hindenburg defences.

Rawlinson therefore faced something of a dilemma. If he continued the slow, deliberate pursuit he could be accused of betraying the French; if he speeded up, his advancing troops faced the prospect of being overwhelmed by counter-attacks supported by batteries safely dug in behind the line. Rawlinson himself was still harbouring ideas of assaulting the line but realised that, given his reduced strength, the likelihood of being allowed to convert this thought into action was, for the time being at least, remote.

Urged on by Haig, Rawlinson laid his plans for early April. He ordered XV Corps to advance and secure a line stretching from Neuville-Bourjonval to the outskirts of Gouzeaucourt. On 29 March the corps cavalry attacked and failed to take Sorel-le-Grand; it, and the neighbouring village of Fins, were finally taken the following day. Their capture allowed the 8th Division to press on and take Dessart Wood, Heudicourt and Révelon. These attacks, which proved to be remarkably successful and with low casualty returns, were assisted by

Trench bridges were manufactured in the rear and brought forward in preparation for an anticipated advance. This bridge is of standard size and construction.

the 20th Division on the left and the 48th Division of III Corps on the right. On 1 April the 48th Division took Peiziere and Epéhy. Three days later the 8th Division supported the 20th Division in an operation on Metz-en-Couture which the official historian later described as a 'very fine attack'.[7]

Metz was, and remains, an unremarkable yet attractive village. It was merely a collection of farms and houses clustered along and around a central crossroads. The inevitable beet factory lay on its south-western edge, with the bulk of the village positioned on a fairly gentle slope rising from Winchester Valley to the south, to Green Jacket Ridge to the north. Further north lies Havrincourt Wood, while about 2000m to the south-east is Gouzeaucourt Wood. The main road between Metz and Gouzeaucourt climbs up to a crossroads east of the

The village of Metz from the Fins Road (D17). This photo shows the land crossed by battalions of the KRRC and RB of the 20th Division when they assaulted the village on 4 April 1917.

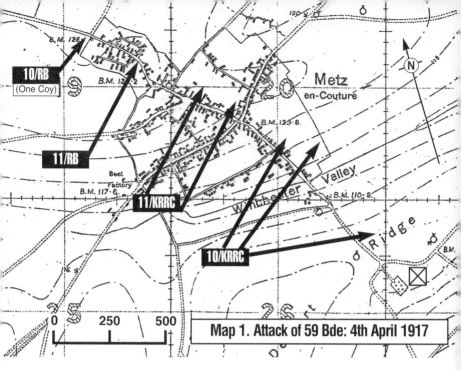

Map 1. Attack of 59 Bde: 4th April 1917

wood known as Queen's Cross. Some 2500m further on the village of Gouzeaucourt lies in a hollow.

At 3.15am on 3 April two patrols from 11/RB, each of one officer and 20 men, crept from their lines a mile distant from Metz; their task was to discover whether the village was still occupied by the enemy. They moved forward towards the housing from the west but their hopes were dashed by a burst of sustained fire from what was certainly an alert garrison. At 1.00am on 4 April, two officers and 26 men from 10/RB, covered by the rifles of C Company, also tried to penetrate the village and met with the same hostile response from machine-gun, rifle and trench-mortar fire. As the cottages and farms appeared to be strongly held, a more deliberate operation was planned to secure its capture.

It was decided that the guns of the entire divisional artillery should be employed to assist 59 Brigade in its assault. On the right,10/KRRC and 11/KRRC would move from Dessart Wood and Fins to capture and hold the village itself. Their advance was scheduled to commence at 2.00pm on 4 April. Eighty-five minutes later on the left of the KRRC, 11/RB, with one company of 10/RB on its left, would attack a trench which ran from the north-western corner of Metz to the south-western corner of Havrincourt Wood. Posts would then be pushed into the wood and held. On the right of the Light Division, 25 Brigade of the 8th

Division was to advance against Gouzeaucourt Wood and the high ground to the south-west of the village. The 2/Berkshire was to attack next to the KRRC, with 2/RB to its right. To assist the Berkshire, two sections of the 25th MGC were instructed to fire a standing barrage over the heads of the advancing troops.

Detailed plans for the assault were hastily prepared and passed on to company commanders. A flexible artillery barrage was originally ordered to commence fire at 2.00pm. It was intended that by a series of coloured rockets infantry commanders would be able to call down local supporting fire or, if necessary, even to bring back the barrage. Orders for 25 Brigade emphasised:

> *The imperative necessity of covering the advance of troops with artillery, machine gun, Lewis gun and rifle fire must be realised by all ranks. Covering fire will be provided prior to each stage of the advance and the smallest units must be on the look out to help neighbouring units in this way.*[8]

As the last batteries had only been positioned minutes before the barrage was due to open, the guns had not had the opportunity to register even on the principal objectives, let alone the smaller targets which the infantry might request. In the event, heavy snow and the resultant poor visibility compelled the gunners to change their plans and revert to a more conventional, timed barrage. The absence of good observation also forced the abandonment of plans to involve a contact aeroplane. Despite these handicaps the infantry formed up on time and on their correct map references. Most battalions ordered their two front companies to advance in two lines at 200 yards distance, with the lines extended to five pace intervals.

At 2.00pm the barrage opened on the area south of the village. The KRRC followed the line of exploding shells and at first met with little opposition from enemy artillery and machine-gun fire. However, as they approached the housing, more intense fire began to sweep through the ranks. By 2.30pm the two right companies of 10/KRRC were heavily engaged by posts to their right, there being no sign of the Berkshire who should have been dealing with them. At 2.35pm, 11/KRRC and two companies of 10/KRRC reached the outskirts of the village and paused for the barrage to lift. Five minutes later they resumed their progress and began to fight their way through the farms and cottages. The left of the 11th Battalion was temporarily held up by strong wire and by fire coming from the trench which ran away towards the western edge of the village; in order to counter this threat, the second line was instructed to swing to the left. The platoons dashed

The open expanse of Green Jacket Ridge between Neuville-Bourjonval and the southern face of Havrincourt Wood (right). 11/RB and one company of 10/RB approached Metz village across this plateau on 4 April 1917.

up the slope, captured the trench but then came under fire themselves from posts established in the north-west corner of the village. A party under Captain Smyth was detached to silence the posts. There was however, growing concern about the situation on the right flank. There was no sign of the Berkshire and when an enemy counter-attack developed from the very positions the Berkshire should by then have secured, one company of 10/RB (brigade reserve) was sent up to form a defensive flank facing east. Eventually touch was gained with the 8th Division and by 3.25pm the entire village, save for a few houses at the northern end, was in British hands. Soon after, 11/RB passed through the KRRC to capture the remainder of the village and dig in to its north.

On the right, the Berkshire had indeed run into difficulties. The two front companies had followed the barrage but were soon held up by wire. The OC B Company on the right despatched a runner to Battalion with the information that he had been unable to get abreast of the wood and was digging in. He was immediately instructed to send a platoon round to the right towards the Rifle Brigade, while the counter-attack company would move up to reinforce his centre. Using the lee of a slight rise as cover, the left company was ordered to work towards the KRRC and to try to enter the wood from its western edge. One company of the 2/Lincolnshire (the support battalion) was sent up to assist in closing the gap developing between the Berkshire and 10/KKRC. Further artillery support was organised but postponed, (so too was the attack by the 2/Lincolnshire), when yellow flares were seen bursting above Gouzeaucourt Wood. These were assumed to have been fired as 'on objective' signals by the 20th Division, but were later reported to have been the flames from sheds burning within the wood. Confusion and rumour reigned until late in the evening when A Company reported that its patrols had entered and were in the process of searching the wood.

Further to the right, 2/RB had also met with considerable opposition. Two companies advanced from the Fins-Gouzeaucourt road with the object of taking the mill and the high ground to the

Site of mill

Taken from beside the D917 on the site of the German strongpoint on Gouzeaucourt Mill. After several attempts 2/RB finally took the position and chased its garrison back to Gouzeaucourt.

south-west of Gouzeaucourt village. Some progress was made until enfilade fire from Gouzeaucourt Wood caused the companies to dig in. Germans in the mill resisted all attempts to oust them during the remainder of the day. In the evening, news arrived that the 20th Division had taken Metz and that the 2/Berkshire was clearing the wood; to conform, riflemen of 2/RB were ordered to take their objectives by standing patrols after dark. In due course half of the Battle Patrol Platoon worked its way onto the high ground to link with the 2/Berkshire while the other half advanced up the main road with the mill as its objective. Again, strong wire and determined resistance frustrated its advance. Thwarted in its attempt, 2/RB paused for the night. Next morning, after a Stokes mortar had landed 30 bombs onto its rapidly disintegrating shell, the strongpoint was rushed. Sergeant Cross of the Battle Patrol Platoon drove the Germans out and down the slope towards Gouzeaucourt. German gunners in the village spotted the chase and began to drop shells onto the riflemen now exposed on the open slope beyond the mill. The patrol withdrew to the crest and occupied the former German trenches. On its right, B Company secured the high ground as far as the Révelon-Gouzeaucourt road.

Nearly four miles to the west, the Rifle Brigade's two New Army battalions advanced at 3.25pm. The troops on the left came under heavy fire from positions in Havrincourt Wood and two platoons from another company were sent up to assist. Those on the right were protected by rising ground for the initial advance and, once the barrage had lifted, successfully rushed their objective. Resistance stiffened as 11/RB worked its way into the Metz. Its companies took Mill Farm on the southern edge of the village and made contact with 11/KRRC. The left flank remained under machine-gun fire coming from the wood but after one failed attempt by Captain Bertie of 11/RB, the guns were finally silenced when their flanks were turned.

With perhaps justifiable pride the chronicler of the KRRC wartime activities went further than the official historian by describing the attack on Metz as 'brilliant'.[9] General Rawlinson sent a message to the division offering his 'hearty congratulations on [its] well deserved success'.[10] Bearing in mind that the weather was against them, that the assaulting troops had already held the front line for eight days and that 25% of them were newly arrived drafts, the attack was a considerable success. The enemy seemed to have been surprised at its audacity and execution for German officers hastily abandoned a meal of hot coffee and English potted meat for the safety of their rear positions. Unsurprisingly, subsequent reports by battalion commanders praised the performance of their troops. Lieutenant-Colonel Haig of the 2/Berkshire thought the operation showed 'excellent leadership on the part of my company commanders'.[11] He singled out the good work done by Lieutenants Hindle and Curtis who 'remained out about 18 hours in close touch with the enemy'.[12] Captain Slade of 11/RB stated 'the action was a fine example of tactical handling of a company and of mutual cooperation and support'.[13] However the cost, especially in the 20th Division, had been heavy. The 10/KRRC had three company commanders and three subalterns killed, with another three wounded. Its sister battalion escaped a little better but still lost two officers and 27 other ranks killed. Thirty-four NCOs and riflemen of 11/RB also lost their lives; another seven died of wounds within two days. In total, 59 Brigade suffered 28% casualties. Many of the dead were subsequently buried in the communal extension cemetery a little to the south of the village. Casualties in 25 Brigade were not so severe. The first return submitted by the Berkshire claimed 16 killed and 30 wounded; this was later revised to a total of three officers wounded, 23 other ranks killed or died of wounds and 22 wounded. These figures later drew the comment that there was 'a curiously large proportion of killed to wounded'.[14] The Rifle Brigade lost ten killed and 25 wounded. A brigade report considered: 'In view of the fact that the enemy held a good position in some strength and that the attacking troops showed up very clearly against the snow [they are] not excessive'.[15]

Despite the success of the operation, XV Corps was still some three miles distant from the outpost positions of the Hindenburg Line. However, Metz and the newly won positions south and west of Gouzeaucourt were within range of German heavy batteries and received their fair share of attention from enemy guns. The day following the attack on Metz, III Corps took the twin villages of Ronssoy and Lempire to the south-east. Their capture allowed Fourth Army's line of resistance to be further advanced. It now ran from Holnon Wood, through Ronssoy, Epéhy and on to Metz. On the left, the

20th Division was in touch with I Anzac Corps of Fifth Army south of Hermies; on the right, III Corps joined with General Humbert's Third Army.

In the early hours of 6 April the 40th Division edged into the gap made by the 8th and 20th Divisions, shifting inward their left and right flanks. It was a front of only some 500m. Relieved of the drudgery of road work, the division rejoined the offensive and their more active comrades of the Old and New Armies. Three days later, and under a moderate barrage, three platoons of the 21/Middlesex advanced towards Dead Man's Corner, north-east of Gouzeaucourt Wood. Having secured the first objective, Second Lieutenant Bryan and one platoon moved towards the second, another cross tracks 600m further on. One section of eight men reached the objective, which lay on the crest of the Beaucamp Ridge, but were caught by machine-gun fire from positions which the artillery had not located or destroyed. All but Bryan were killed. One platoon of D Company was sent up to outflank the machine gun; when its crew saw the danger, it retired in the direction of Villers-Plouich. This minor operation cost the Middlesex 27 killed and 38 wounded. The casualty list might have been higher were it not for the work done by Captain P. Caffikin RAMC, of the 136th Field Ambulance. When he visited the HQ of the Middlesex near Metz cemetery, Caffikin discovered that the regimental medical officer had not arrived at the battalion's aid post. He therefore took it upon himself to organise the bearers and acted as RMO until all wounded were evacuated. The 13/Yorkshire, also of 121 Brigade, had been

Troops at rest were employed in a multitude of tasks. Here men of the KOYLI fuse Stokes mortar bombs in October 1917.

The ground traversed by the 2/East Lancashire and 2/Sherwood Foresters as they approached Gouzeaucourt in a snow storm, 12 April 1917. Gonnelieu village is on the right, the trees of La Vacquerie, centre, and Gouzeaucourt church left. By 1918 the area closest to the camera lay just to the rear of the British Battle Zone.

slightly involved in support to the Middlesex and, although only suffering a few wounded, had lost Lieutenant Charles Jennings to one of the many snipers operating from Gouzeaucourt. The wounded were evacuated via the 136th Field Ambulance which had, during Caffikin's absence, moved up from Fins.

The next major obstacle confronting XV Corps was the substantial village of Gouzeaucourt. The built-up area lies on a slope falling to the railway on its eastern side, with the old Roman road between Péronne and Cambrai passing through the centre. Smaller roads connect the village with Villers-Guislain beyond the Quentin Ridge and with Villers-Plouich and Trescault to the north and north-west. In April 1917 most of Gouzeaucourt's buildings were still reasonably intact. These would provide good positions should the enemy decide to stand and fight within its streets.

Anticipating that the Germans would stand, Lieutenant-General Du Cane instructed the 8th Division to undertake an operation which would eject the enemy from their prepared positions. Attacks to the south were to continue while XV Corps used a short respite to consolidate its new line and to reconnoitre the approaches to Gouzeaucourt. In the dark, sleeting night of 9 April, Lieutenant Thompson and ten men of the 2/East Lancashire crept from their snow filled shell holes and advanced cautiously into No Man's Land. Their intention was to gain contact with the enemy believed to be strongly entrenched in Gauche Wood. No shots were heard by their fellows and no bodies were discovered the following day. It was assumed that the entire patrol had been surprised and captured. The weather remained foul, heavy driving snow replacing the earlier sleet. To help the infantry maintain direction in the murk, the artillery was to fire on fixed positions; the shell bursts would thus act as markers to the following troops. When the infantry reached their objectives they were instructed to fire rockets as the signal for the barrage to lift onto the next targets. On the far right, the 2/West Yorkshire of 23 Brigade was

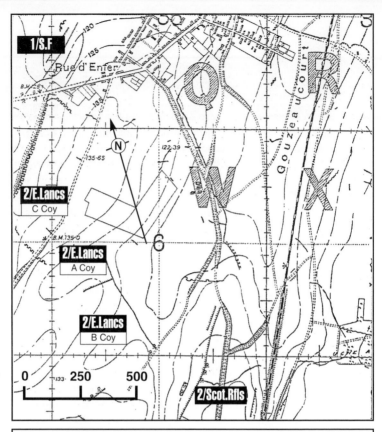

Map 2. 8th Division's attack on Gouzeaucourt: 12th April 1917

to attack towards the right of Gauche Wood, while three companies of the 2/Scottish Rifles were to cross the railway line and advance up the slope to clear the wood and Quentin Mill to its north. With two companies of the 2/Middlesex in support, they would therefore approach Gouzeaucourt from its eastern edge. The 2/East Lancashire, with two companies up to follow the Battle Patrol Platoon acting as advanced guard, was to move directly upon Gouzeaucourt from the south-west. Two companies of the 1/Sherwood Foresters, with their HQ at Queen's Cross, were to advance down the slope and approach the village from the west.

The initial bombardment was timed to last only ten minutes; it was then to lift onto the fixed positions and remain on them until the infantry advised otherwise. The evening of 12 April was heralded by a ferocious blizzard. This was somewhat of a mixed blessing as, although unpleasant for the troops, the snow blew onto the backs of the attackers and made German observation of their progress that much more difficult. At zero the 1/Sherwood Foresters moved off with 'great dash',[16] sweeping aside the German outposts west of Devillers Farm. Closer to the village, the Battle Patrol Platoon encountered strong wire and met with considerable resistance. Hacking their way through the wire, the Foresters surged into the village streets and secured their objectives which lay to the west of the central road.

The 2/East Lancashire occupied a front of about 1500m, with its left upon the Fins Road. The Battle Patrol Platoon led the advance upon the village, with the centre moving along the Révelon road. The two following companies entered the village and established posts along the railway and west of the station. The snow evidently helped the attackers as the Germans initially failed to appreciate the strength and organisation of the assault. Some sporadic resistance was encountered in the early stages but the enemy soon withdrew and contented themselves with shelling their evacuated positions.

To the right of the East Lancashire, the Scottish Rifles followed the railway, passed through the eastern edge of the village and dug in to the east of the station. B Company actually advanced too far and was busily entrenching on a line well beyond its objective when Major Stirling, the second in command, appeared and took the company back to its intended position. The battalion had sustained only one casualty, and he had remained at duty. The following day C Company attacked again, on this occasion with a section of the 23rd MGC in close support. The Rifles soon came across a strong belt of wire and an enemy machine gun which opened up from a range of only 25m. The attackers fell flat and a message was sent back ordering up the machine-gun section. Lance Corporal Wood mounted his gun on the the left flank of the Rifles' second wave but realised that he could not open fire without hitting the prostrate Scots. With the assistance of Sergeant Page, the two NCOs carried the mounted gun to the centre of the first wave and engaged the enemy weapon at almost point-blank range. Wood fired off one belt and called for more to be brought forward. None arrived so he went back himself to bring up a box, loaded a belt and reopened fire. The enemy gun was subdued and the Rifles surged forward to secure their objective.

On 14 April, having cleared Gauche Wood, 23 Brigade pressed on towards Villers-Guislain. For three uncomfortable and trying weeks, XV Corps had moved forward with resolution and flexibility. Its divisions were now almost within striking distance of the final hurdle - the outposts of the Hindenburg Line itself. There remained one last string of ridges to climb and secure before they could look upon their goal. What the troops did not yet know was how much further they would be required to advance. The Battle of Arras had opened to the north and communications back across the devastated zone were not yet sufficiently repaired to permit the volumes of traffic a major assault against the Hindenburg position would require. The troops might assume that they would be ordered to make one more bound to secure the ridges in front of the outpost line but, at least while elements of First, Third and Fifth Armies continued their thrusts in the direction of Douai and Cambrai, that they would be unlikely to mount a major attack against the main enemy positions. They would certainly anticipate, however, having to maintain strong pressure on the Germans in the hope of drawing away enemy forces from the Arras front.

NOTES
1. War diary 13/Yorkshire. WO.95.2616
2. War diary 181 Bde RFA. WO.95.2598
3. Ibid
4. *Official History of the Great War, 1917*. Vol.I p.123
5. Ibid
6. Ibid, p.123-4
7. Ibid, p.159
8. War diary 2/Berkshire. WO.95.1729
9. *Annals of the KRRC. Vol.V* p.188
10. V. Inglefield, *The History of the Twentieth (Light) Division*, p.133
11. War diary 2/Berkshire, op.cit.
12. Ibid
13. War diary 11/Rifle Brigade. WO.95.2116
14. F. Petrie, *The Royal Berkshire Regiment*, p.89
15. War diary 2/Berkshire, op.cit.
16. H.Wylly, *The Sherwood Foresters in the Great War*, p.44

A German photo of Gouzeaucourt taken before April 1917. The church was used as a hospital and the nearest house as a canteen.   (IWM Q45364)

Chapter Two

THE CAPTURE OF VILLERS-PLOUICH AND THE RIDGES

Final preparations for the assaults on the villages immediately in front of the Hindenburg Line began once Gouzeaucourt and Gauche Wood had been secured. The 8th Division was to go for Villers-Guislain and Gonnelieu, the 40th Division for Villers-Plouich and Beaucamp and the 20th for Trescault. Before the villages themselves could be assaulted, the British positions had first to be worked forward another few hundred metres. The initial moves were made by XV Corps on 21 April. Simultaneous attacks were made by the 8th Division on Gonnelieu and the 20th Division towards Trescault. The historian of the 40th Division described the terrain over which his division was to attack as:

> ...open and undulating, but intersected by numerous so-called ravines characteristic of this sector of the front. There was little or no cultivation, but the grass was thick and high. The villages were mostly standing, as the enemy was using them as strong points, while the ground was fairly free from shell holes and remained so for a considerable time afterwards...All cross roads had been "cratered" by the enemy. Taken as a whole it was good fighting country, with natural cover and good observation. No Man's Land was very wide in places, "and extremely interesting owing to the long grass," as one idealist puts it.[1]

At 4.20am the 2/Lincolnshire, with 2/RB in support, fought its way into Gonnelieu, reaching its eastern end almost an hour later. The Rifle Brigade was held up for a time by fire from the chateau but a patrol of the 19/RWF led by Second Lieutenant Dunn outflanked the troublesome machine gun and allowed the remainder of the village to be secured.

On the left, two patrols of 12/KRRC went forward at 4.20am and established posts on the hillside to the south-west of Trescault, in touch with the 40th Division on their right. The patrols came under shell fire but at 10.30am Second Lieutenant Thornton-Smith took four scouts into the village and dug in at its southern end. The bulk of the village was known to be strongly held. Thornton-Smith (who was to be killed in August 1917) discovered the enemy to be digging a trench among a collection of farm buildings known as Bilhem, 600m to the east of the village. The enemy was holding the houses and cottages in force but by

11.00pm Lieutenant Sampson of D Company had worked forward sufficiently to place posts at the central crossroads. The following morning Sampson sent patrols to follow the redoubtable Thornton-Smith as he progressed further into what approximated to a built-up area. As no fire came from the houses it was assumed the Germans had evacuated their positions during the night. When, however, the Rifles came in view of the defenders ensconced in Bilhem, they came under intense fire. The patrol withdrew to find shelter in nearby cottages and consolidated. Thornton-Smith, whose 'control of these operations was so decisive that by 9.30am...the village was cleared of the enemy'[2] was awarded the DSO. Progress in the centre of the Corps was slower than that made by the KRRC. It soon became clear that the 40th Division had been delayed and that although the 20th Division now held Trescault, it would be required to press on and secure the enemy strong points in and around Bilhem. Until they were taken, enemy machine-gun fire would make the the 40th Division's precarious hold on Beaucamp untenable.

The area of assault designated to the 40th Division stretched from the Péronne-Cambrai road to Beaucamp Ridge and Trescault Spur. 119 Brigade, with the 19/RWF on the right and the 12/SWB on the left, was to take Fifteen Ravine – in reality more a depression never more than ten feet deep rather than a ravine – and the spur which ran north-west of Gonnelieu. On its left, 120 Brigade, with the 13/East Surrey and the 11/King's Own in the van, was to attack the high ground which overlooked Villers-Plouich from the west. Preliminary measures began on 15 April when the Divisional artillery commenced wire-cutting in front of Villers-Plouich. There was concern over the state of the guns, those of 181 Brigade RFA, for example, being reported as 'worn out'.[3] Arrangements were in hand to remove and overhaul them but the battery was told to ensure that any guns taken to the repair shops should be back in position and ready to fire by the night of 19-20 April.

In the early hours of 18 April, the South Wales Borderers relieved the 12/Suffolk while the 19/RWF slotted into the front and outpost positions to the right of the Borderers. Lieutenant-Colonel Pope of the SWB, who was later to have a long communication trench named in his

Taken from the D29 on the crest of Beaucamp Ridge, Beaucamp village is on the right and the trees on the site of Bilhem Farm, left.

Charing Cross   Bilhem   Trescault Spur   Beaucamp

honour, ripped his cheek on some wire when out on a reconnaissance and was evacuated to a CCS. Two companies were sent into the outposts, each with a further platoon in close support. During the darkness of the succeeding night, Lieutenant Osborn took a fighting patrol to investigate Fifteen Ravine, discovering it to be strongly held. On the following day Lieutenant Williams crawled from his outpost position and made a careful daylight patrol of the land lying in front of the ravine. He plotted several snipers' posts for what was termed 'further treatment'.[4] The right company of the 19/RWF pushed forward a little in support of the 8th Division's ultimately unsuccessful attack on Gonnelieu, but with its flank in the air, was later withdrawn to conform. On 20 April further progress was made when posts were established in the quarry which lay just east of the railway beyond Gouzeaucourt station. The Borderers reported their front to be quiet and took advantage of the lull in German shelling to put out some wire. The battalion knew that its attack was timed for 4.20am, the same hour as the rest of XV Corps would be going over the top. During the night Battalion HQ moved up to a hole in the bank which lined the Gouzeaucourt-Trescault road; the artillery continued to fire a slow programme designed to blow gaps in the opposing wire and the machine-gunners fired sporadic bursts towards the enemy lines and rear areas. In the front positions, the companies formed up, checked their equipment for the umpteenth time and waited for the whistles.

At 3.15am the leading waves were given the correct intervals of thirty paces and ordered to lie down above the parapet to await the barrage. In addition to their normal fighting order, each man carried two Mills bombs, sandbags and 50 extra rounds of small-arms ammunition. Those sections detailed as mopper-ups were warned to pay particular attention to the dugouts suspected of lining the ravine and the shell holes in front which were assumed to double as snipers' posts. As soon as they moved off the leading waves came under shrapnel and HE fire from a German counter-barrage. The enemy took a particular interest in the area which housed battalion HQ and to the front British trenches. As strong machine-gun and rifle fire continued to originate from positions in the ravine, it appeared that the British barrage had failed to neutralise a number of its defenders. For about 15 minutes the assaulting waves were checked and sought cover. Small parties eventually worked their way to the flank and at 5.15am the ravine was entered. The enemy then immediately evacuated their positions and retired towards Villers-Plouich. A Company on the right crossed the Gouzeaucourt-Villers-Plouich road and advanced a further

300m before encountering strong wire. About the road the ravine peters out and lacks clear definition; a hasty conference of company officers checked their maps and the land and decided they had progressed too far. They withdrew their platoons and took up positions on what they considered to be the objectives. Captain Whitworth was awarded the MC for the manner in which he commanded his company during the manoeuvre.

Sections searched dugouts and shell holes for prisoners, souvenirs and booby traps. Several Germans gave themselves up and from their statements it seems that the ravine had been garrisoned by about 150 men. The defenders of a number of strong points which lay between the old British line and the ravine, and which had been by-passed during the attack, made their unwelcome presence felt but were soon dispersed by bombers and Lewis-gun teams. Germans in three positions continued to fire into the rear of the left platoons and the carrying parties which followed behind. One platoon of the support battalion, the 18/Welch, under the command of the Borderers' Intelligence Officer, Second Lieutenant Williams, was despatched to deal with them. The posts were eventually silenced and more prisoners taken. German fire, largely from the high ground to the south-west of Villers-Plouich continued to harass the new occupants of the ravine until the trench which was the source of the discomfort was finally taken by a platoon of the Borderers. Another troublesome machine gun was knocked out by the artillery, much to the satisfaction of the observing and suffering infantry. One party of about 15 Germans was observed casting away equipment as it bolted down the slope towards Villers-Plouich; it had Lewis guns turned on it and another group, seen fleeing from snipers' posts in front of the village, was similarly handled. Sniper fire from posts on the slope east of the village continued to disturb the entrenching Borderers and the carrying parties bringing forward engineering stores and ammunition across the old No Man's Land. One party from the 119th Trench Mortar Battery was singled out by the Borderers' diarist for special mention. Frequently under shell and small-arms fire, the party worked all day carrying material from the brigade to battalion dumps.

The other attacking battalions had an easier time than the Borderers. The Welch Fusiliers, with two companies forward, had taken their objectives and were consolidating by 5.15am. The greatest excitement came when Second Lieutenant Dunn's party attacked the strong point north of Gonnelieu at the request of 2/RB. To assist the RB in gaining their objective, the Fusiliers, who immediately dubbed the ridge they

Fifteen Ravine   Beaucamp   Villers-Plouich

he exposed approaches to Villers-Plouich the road is the D89. The photo is taken from here Fern Trench, the British front line during the summer of 1917, met the Cambrai ad on Cemetery Ridge

now occupied Fusilier Ridge, were provided with a section of three guns of the 119th MGC; another section of the company covered Fifteen Ravine for the SWB. On the front of 120 Brigade the 13/East Surrey had advanced to occupy a line running roughly from the western end of Fifteen Ravine to a sunken lane leaving the Gouzeaucourt-Trescault road to Beaucamp. Patrols had actually reached the battalion's objective shortly after midnight, so when zero came at 4.20am, the two leading companies had little to do. With virtually no resistance, the battalion had only three men wounded. On the left of the Surreys, and despite machine-gun fire from Trescault, the King's Own reached the high ground of the Trescault Spur. So straightforward was the advance that three platoons surged beyond their objective and, until recalled, chased the retreating Germans towards Beaucamp.

Apart from the casualties sustained by the SWB, the day had been a remarkably bloodless one for the 40th Division. Casualties in 120 Brigade were slight, while the total in 119 Brigade amounted to 157. The RWF lost fewer than a dozen killed and about 40 wounded. The Borderers lost three officers, including Captain Morris, and 22 other ranks killed. A further five men were to die of wounds and there were five officers and over 50 men wounded. The Borderers counted 34 dead Germans and between them the two attacking battalions of 119 Brigade took 40 prisoners. The division's chronicler attributed the overall low casualty list to the fact that the assaulting troops formed up in advance of their forward posts. When the enemy barrage came down it fell on the front positions rather than on the leading waves. Most of the casualties were therefore sustained after the troops had taken their objectives and whilst in the process of consolidating.

The 8th, 40th and 20th Divisions were in position to launch what for the time being was destined to be Fourth Army's final major thrust towards the Hindenburg Line. The 8th Division was to hold fast in Gonnelieu while the 40th was to advance further up Fusilier Ridge and

43

gain a foothold on Welsh and Highland Ridges. The two villages of Villers-Plouich and Beaucamp were also to fall within its remit. On the left, the 20th Division was to complete the capture of the crest of the spur east of Trescault by seizing the hotly disputed area of Bilhem; the high ground facing the village from the north-west had been secured by 12/RB and 6/KSLI on the night of 22 April. That same night, a patrol of 13 men of the 11/King's Own, led by Second Lieutenant Cooke, crept from a captured German trench on the Trescault Spur near Charing Cross and advanced cautiously towards Beaucamp. Fire from the village prevented the patrol from getting further than 50m east of Charing Cross. Cooke decided to withdraw. Bringing with them the body of one comrade and assisting four wounded, the patrol regained its own trench. During the night the 14/Argyll & Sutherland Highlanders, which was shortly to lead the assault on Beaucamp, relieved the King's Own in the front line.

Also on the move that night was the 136th Field Ambulance. Its members had been busy building patient accommodation at Fins, but on 22-23 April parties were sent forward to establish regimental aid posts and relay posts along the tracks and roads leading towards Villers-Plouich. A little forward of the orderlies the SWB took up positions in the new line of resistance. The battalion, which was to remain in the line as brigade reserve, came under fire from the crest of Borderer Ridge. At the same time the 19/RWF on its right was ordered to move to Fifteen Ravine; the Fusiliers were to act as support battalion to the two assaulting units of 119 Brigade, the 18th and 17/Welch. These two battalions were ordered to establish strong points as far forward as the minor road running between Gonnelieu and Villers-Plouich, roughly on top of Fusilier Ridge. The battalions were each to have the support of four guns of the 119th TMB and ten guns of the 119th MGC. Four of the Vickers were to fire north-east from the Cambrai road, sweeping the ground across which the Glamorgans were to advance; another six guns were dug in on Borderer Ridge and were to provide overhead fire with specified lifts from the eastern edge of Farm Ravine towards La Vacquerie. The crews were warned not to traverse their guns and to pay special attention to cover the left flank of the brigade as it approached the spur to the south-east of Villers-

Beaucamp village from the west. In April 1917 and September 1918 British battalions of the 40th and 5th Divisions suffered severely in their attempts to cross the fields and enter the village. The trees of La Vacquerie are on the right.

Plouich. With the infantry providing labour, Major Harrison ordered all guns to be dug in and camouflaged. Harrison inspected the finished work, expressed some dissatisfaction at several of the positions but conceded that all guns were invisible from a distance of 50 yards. The company's six reserve guns were positioned a little to the north-east of Gouzeaucourt.

The task of 120 Brigade on the left was thought to be more demanding than that faced by their Welsh colleagues of 119 Brigade. Villers-Plouich was to be taken by the 13/East Surrey and Beaucamp by the 14/A&SH. Behind these two assaulting battalions the 14/HLI was in support to the Surreys and three companies of the King's Own were in support to the Argylls. Eight guns of the 120th MGC were to fire overhead barrages and parties of RE and Pioneers of the 12/Yorkshire were ready to carry, consolidate and dig communication trenches across the former No Man's Land.

By the early hours of 24 April all battalions and units were in position and waiting for zero. The divisional artillery had continued to fire a regular programme of wire-cutting and gaps were known to exist in several places. The night was dry, with the snow of the earlier days now thawed. The ground was wet and the air chilly but the division was confident that it could take its objectives. With the 8th Division on Cemetery Ridge, the right flank was secure; the left was rather more problematical. It was anticipated that Villers-Plouich and Beaucamp would not in themselves pose too many difficulties, but the high ground to the north could. Until Bilhem fell to the 20th Division any penetration of Beaucamp by the 40th would be observed from the ruins of the farm buildings. Enfilade fire could be brought down upon Beaucamp and make its possession by 120 Brigade expensive.

On the right, the 18/Welch advanced before the official zero hour. The battalion moved up from the quarry east of Fifteen Ravine and pushed out covering parties towards the objective. Shortly after 2am four strong points had been established and, after the barrage opened at 4.15am, two companies pressed on and made contact with the 17/Welch on their left. The task was achieved with the loss of three wounded. The only real excitement came later in the morning when 27 Germans who had been passed over during the advance were rounded up in Farm Ravine.

The objective of the 17/Welch was the high ground south-east of Villers-Plouich. The barrage fell on the enemy trenches and their protecting wire which, although damaged, was later discovered to be thicker than anticipated. In most places it consisted of one belt 25 feet

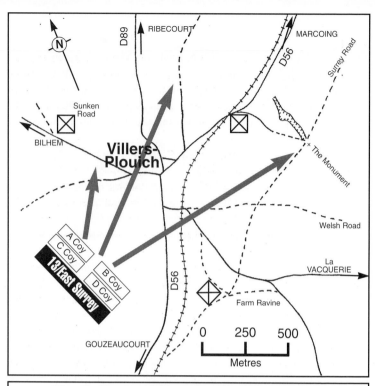

N

D89 ↑ RIBECOURT

MARCOING

D56

Surrey Road

Sunken Road

BILHEM

⊠

Villers-Plouich

⊠

The Monument

Welsh Road

A Coy
C Coy

B Coy
D Coy

13/East Surrey

D56

La VACQUERIE

⊕

Farm Ravine

0   250   500

GOUZEAUCOURT

Metres

Map 3. Attack on Villers-Plouich: 24th April 1917

deep, supported in some sections by a second belt ten metres to its rear. The true extent of the wire had only been realised by the artillery during the previous day. Maps were issued on 23 April and until then it was not known that a second belt existed. Remedial lane cutting was observed to be largely disappointing, the only significant gaps being blown on the slopes around the Monument. The 18-pounders of B/181 battery RFA were firing at the slopes from south of Queen's Cross, with C/181 positioned just to its north. The range began at 4000m and would ultimately increase to 6000m. Forward Observation Officers established good posts during the night 23-24 April but visibility around zero was so bad that the guns fired with little confirmation of their effect. The creeping barrage was timed to progress at a rate of 100m in four minutes; it would then remain on the German second line while the infantry consolidated on the first.

The enemy counter-barrage passed over the heads of 119 Brigade and caused little damage. By 4.45am, one of the 17/Welch's support companies reported that it held Surrey Road near the Monument but, one hour later, C Company reported that it was held up by wire in front of its objective a little east of Surrey Road. The OC D Company saw a gap in the wire being utilised by B Company and took his men through. By 9.40am all objectives were reported to be in the battalion's possession and consolidation was in hand. The advance, which according to the battalion's adjutant was made 'as coolly and steadily as if on a parade ground',[5] resulted in the death of Captain Young and 27 other ranks.[6] A total of just over 60 wounded completed the initial casualty return. The operation had gone very well but, on the left, things were not as satisfactory and Division warned 119 Brigade that it might be required to attack Beaucamp from the south. Accordingly, the 19/RWF, which had two companies in Fifteen Ravine and the other two in the sunken Gouzeaucourt-Trescault road just north of Gouzeaucourt, was warned for a move. The 13/Yorkshire was ordered to be ready to move up and occupy the main line of resistance once it was vacated by the Fusiliers and the Borderers. In the event the warning orders were not executed as Division decided that a further attack on Beaucamp should be postponed until the 20th Division could assist. Until 10.30am, when it became clear that the village was in British hands, there was confusion in the gun lines as to who held Villers-Plouich. The batteries spent the remainder of the day firing barrages at varying rates to relieve pressure on the newly captured positions while consolidation was effected. Assistance from heavy artillery was frequently asked for and afforded.

The village and Highland Ridge beyond had been the objective of the 13/East Surrey. The battalion formed up with 24 officers and 600 other ranks in a new trench which ran north-west from Fifteen Ravine. The two assaulting companies were to be B on the right, supported by D, and A on the left, with C in support. At 4.14am the four leading waves advanced under the barrage and at 5.30am, after a short struggle, entered the village. The German counter-barrage was described as 'very erratic'[7] and, although causing little damage to the Surrey, did knock over some of the HLI to the rear. There was some resistance as the battalion approached the village but the 'concentrated fire of Lewis guns and daring attacks by bombers'[8] overcame the garrisons of several machine-gun posts.

Once the outer perimeter defences had been penetrated the assaulting waves divided into three groups. Captain Crocker took the right party towards the ravine some 700m east of the village. Intense fire greeted the attempt but the group eventually reached the ravine, albeit with the loss of Crocker. It was here, whilst in charge of two Lewis guns, that Corporal Foster and Lance Corporal Reed performed acts of outstanding bravery. The NCOs attacked several machine guns

With the slope of Fusilier Ridge on the right, the church and cottages of La Vacquerie can be seen clustered on the eastern slope of Welsh Ridge. The embankment (left) follows the line of Village Road.

which were holding up the advance, knocked them out and captured the teams. Foster was later awarded the VC and Reed the DCM. To their left, the centre party passed through the village and climbed the slope of Highland Ridge. The extreme left party took a German strong point a little north-west of the village on the sunken road running up to Beaucamp, capturing over 100 prisoners in the process. Any further advance was abandoned when it became obvious that Beaucamp was still in enemy hands. For the time being all the Surreys could do was to consolidate and throw out a defensive flank to cover Beaucamp and the northern face of Highland Ridge.

At 5.45am a message from the East Surrey requesting assistance arrived at the HQ of the 14/HLI. Coming under shell fire as they moved forward to the cross roads west of the village, the Scots took up positions covering the several roads and tracks heading into the village. The move coincided with the conclusion of the British barrage and the opening of a very heavy bombardment by enemy howitzers targeted at the centre and right parties of the East Surrey. At the ravine east of the village Lieutenant Hann, to whom command had devolved on Crocker's death, had withdrawn the most advanced troops to the eastern outskirts of the village and established Lewis gun posts to command its approaches. By 7.05am one company of the HLI had braved the shell fire to assist the left of the Surreys and by 8.12am a strong point east of the cemetery was established and the ravine secured. For his command and gallantry during this supporting operation Lieutenant-Colonel Dick of the HLI was awarded l'Ordre de Léopold to go with his DSO.

The Germans, not yet content to leave 120 Brigade in peace, opened a furious bombardment of the village at about 8.30am. Casualties occurred among the troops attempting to consolidate and among the carrying parties bringing forward the stores and equipment. The intense area bombardment lasted for nearly six hours; fire then slackened and concentrated instead on the village and its exits. While the 13/East Surrey was allowed to seek whatever shelter the forward positions already possessed, the HLI was allotted the task of constructing defensive posts a little further to the rear. The Surrey, which had lost three officers and over 25 killed and about 170 wounded, was later praised by the CO of the HLI for the 'rapidity and dash'[9] which had taken them into and beyond Villers-Plouich. The battalion had captured over 300 Germans and ten machine guns and, in addition to Foster's VC and Reed's DCM, five other men were awarded the MM.[10] Further to the left, however, success was proving far more difficult to achieve.

During the night of 23-24 April the Argyll & Sutherland Highlanders had sent out several patrols to investigate the wire running across the front of Beaucamp. The patrols reported the wire to be strong and that the enemy was fully alert. The divisional artillery was ordered to concentrate upon the areas where the wire was thought to be thickest; if it was considered necessary, 120 Brigade could request the help of XV Corps heavy artillery. In addition, eight guns of the 120th MGC were to target the area between Boar Copse and Bilhem and the crest of Highland Ridge behind Beaucamp. Sappers of the 229th Field Company established forward dumps just behind the British front lines and were instructed to send forward consolidation parties once the village and the high ground had been captured. To help with the task of securing the gains, one company of the 11/King's Own was to advance with the Argylls and act as garrisons at strong points to be established at Charing Cross and, when possible, to push down Beaucamp Valley. Finally, troops were warned to look out for contact aircraft, identifiable by black streamers attached to their wings and by klaxon horns.

Having drawn SAA, picks and shovels, the two assaulting companies were in position by 3.45am. When the barrage opened at

The ravine at the north-eastern end of Villers-Plouich. Corporal Foster won the VC and Lance Corporal Reed the DCM when the 13/East Surrey attacked German machine-gun nests in the ravine. It was later riven by British dugouts.

ATTACK

4.15am the companies moved off and immediately came under shell fire from the German counter-bombardment. D Company under Captain Mackie discovered the wire to be still intact, but with the help of wire cutters managed to hack its way through. Fire, particularly from Bilhem on its left front, continued to pour into the ranks. The Germans were clearly expecting the attack but, with a rush and hurling bombs as they went, D Company dispersed the enemy positioned in a trench traversing the fields in front of the village. Platoons of the 14/HLI and the 11/King's Own were left to consolidate the position while the Highlanders moved on towards the second objective, Beaucamp itself.

Followed by B Company under Captain Miller, at 4.45am D Company pushed on and into the village. There was comparatively little resistance from the enemy within the buildings but when the two companies ventured beyond the cottages and into the fields to the east, withering fire from the left tore into their flank. Although it was still only half light, German machine-gunners in Bilhem and in the shell holes and slit trenches on the slope of Beaucamp Valley, spotted the Argylls as they emerged from the ruins. Their combined fire soon brought the stuttering advance to a halt. Second Lieutenant Runciman of D Company went forward to establish Lewis gun posts in the eastern-most buildings and was wounded almost immediately. His wounds were bound up but the young man refused to be evacuated, electing instead to remain with his men and to encourage them to

Map 4. Attack on Beaucamp: 24th April 1917

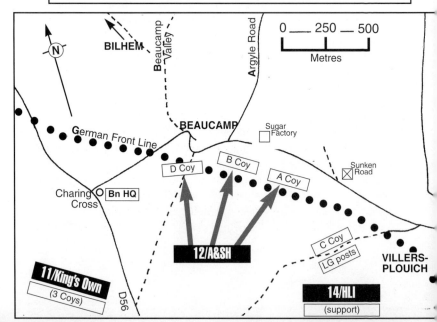

sustain rapid fire in the direction of the German machine guns. Runciman died of his wounds shortly afterwards and, with Captain Mackie and Second Lieutenants Walter and Law already wounded, command of D Company devolved upon Corporal Johnston.

A message was finally received at the gun lines requesting the artillery to concentrate its fire on the machine-gun posts in Bilhem. The guns responded but with apparently little effect. Like D Company, B, which was attempting to seek cover among the disintegrating cottages of Beaucamp, was suffering badly. Captain Miller and Second Lieutenant Biggart were wounded and Second Lieutenant Humphreys was killed. The beleaguered company, hanging on as best it could, watched in horror as the two supporting companies attempted to get through the wire. Despite the best efforts of the Highlanders' Lewis guns to silence it, deadly enfilade fire continued to come from Bilhem and the slope below. In the maelstrom through which the two supporting companies attempted to pass, two officers were wounded and Captain Urquhart and Lieutenants Lawson and Forbes were all killed. By dawn the situation was becoming critical. The early light helped the artillery spotters to identify the enemy positions more clearly and the guns were again brought into action. However, with three company commanders out of action, and all four companies spread over a wide area, the Argylls desperately needed to regroup. In order to provide a covering screen, Captain Keddie and C Company's Lewis guns succeded in manning the sunken lane which crossed the fields towards Villers-Plouich. Simultaneously the remnant of A Company withdrew from the eastern side of Beaucamp to a position immediately south of the village. Touch was gained with C Company and a rough line of unconnected shell holes was established. This line soon came under heavy shell fire from 5.9-inch guns.

Next came a period of torrid endurance. Several NCOs, including Sergeant Lambie and Corporal Couper, were later singled out for special mention. Until they were both killed these men crawled from shell hole to shell hole encouraging and calming their men. Sergeant MacNeil and members of A Company collected shovels and picks and began, despite the shells howling around them, to begin consolidating the line south of the village. Shunning cover, Second Lieutenant Shaw of the 11/King's Own went out to bring in some of the wounded Argylls lying on the left flank, while Second Lieutenant Kilgour, the Argylls' Signalling Officer, braved the shells and sniper fire to establish a telephone line between Battalion HQ at Charing Cross and Captain Keddie's position nearer the village. Three of Kilgour's linesmen were knocked over while attempting to keep the line connected. Several runners then ran the gauntlet between the forward positions and HQ, bringing with them map references of the enemy machine-gun posts. Lieutenant McCrow, bringing one such message himself, arrived at HQ just as a 77mm shell landed in the shell hole which constituted the command post. Before rejoining his platoon, McCrow made himself useful by binding the wounds of those injured by the explosion.

One company of the 11/King's Own was sent forward to strengthen the left and, despite the now full light, miraculously suffered little from the German barrage sweeping the open ground. The fire did however betray the position of the enemy guns and, with a telephone link now in operation, the artillery and Lewis guns redoubled their efforts. The fire forced several Germans to break cover above Beaucamp Valley; about 25 of them were shot down by Lewis guns before they could reach safety. This renewal of activity coincided with the order to 119 Brigade warning that it might be required to carry Beaucamp from the direction of Villers-Plouich.

Shelling, including a German box barrage around Villers-Plouich which aroused fears of a major counter-attack, continued during the remainder of the morning. No German attack materialised and Lance Corporal Crauford used whatever lulls there were to get the isolated groups of D Company back into the main battalion position a few hundred metres west and south of the village. About midday the Argylls cautiously pushed three strong patrols into the village from their advanced positions. The patrols drew fire from both flanks and from the high ground behind but it appeared that the ruins themselves were no longer occupied. The patrols withdrew to their earlier positions and reported their intelligence. Another attempt was made two hours later but during the intervening period the enemy had filtered back into the cottages and once again repulsed the Highlanders.

An artillery duel, which kept the Argylls' stretcher-bearers and the reserve bearers of the battalion band busy until the evening, recommenced soon after. Members of A and C Companies attempted to deepen and improve the advanced trench while survivors of D and B occupied the old German trench a little to the rear. Corps realised that unless Bilhem was taken any further effort against Beaucamp would result in yet more slaughter. Accordingly, the 20th Division was ordered to advance from Trescault and secure the troublesome collection of buildings. Once that had been achieved, the 11/King's

Own, which was to relieve the Argylls, would at 4.15am on 25 April launch another assault on Beaucamp.

The 20th Division had not been totally inactive during 24 April. Supported from time to time by the divisional batteries, 12/RB had confined itself to training its Lewis guns in Trescault on Bilhem. Their fire was intended as a bluff to convince the garrison that an attack was imminent. In order to ascertain some idea of the German positions, Second Lieutenant Benson of 6/Ox & Bucks reconnoitred beyond Trescault. When he failed to return it was assumed he had lost his way and had been killed.[11] As a preliminary measure a patrol of one officer and 19 men of the battalion's D Company cleared the civilian cemetery north of the Ribécourt road; the group subsequently came under the orders of the CO of 12/KRRC. It was to this battalion that the task of taking Bilhem was entrusted. Three companies moved up at 9pm: D Company on the left was in touch with the Ox & Bucks in the cemetery; A Company a little below the crest of the Gouzeaucourt road south-west of Trescault and C Company in support. Battalion HQ was sited in a ravine to the right of the Trescault-Metz road. At 11pm the artillery, consisting of 91 Field Artillery Brigade, three 18-pounder batteries of 92 Brigade and a heavy battery, commenced fire. The artillery was supplemented by the guns of the 60th TMB; the mortars heralded the bombardment by dropping 120 rounds onto Bilhem in a five minute period. The artillery barrage initially concentrated on the enemy trench in front of Bilhem and was then scheduled to creep back 100 yards in two minutes. At 11.02pm D and A Companies of the Rifles advanced. A Company quickly captured the German trench but in its enthusiasm went on too far. Seeing the danger that a counter-attack could pose to the advancing company, Second Lieutenant McDonald, in command of C Company, took his men forward to fill the positions which A Company should have consolidated. On the left, D Company went through to Bilhem without opposition and reorganised itself among the tumbled buildings. Less than 25 minutes after the operation began, and for a cost of only nine wounded, all objectives had been taken. Two companies of the 6/Ox & Bucks were sent up to provide close support while the Rifles dug in.

The enemy was not yet finished with the Rifles; at 3am he opened up a heavy bombardment of Bilhem, killing and wounding over 30 men. When B Company came up from reserve in Havrincourt Wood, intense fire prevented it from consolidating the lane running from Bilhem to Beaucamp and it was forced to retire. About noon however, when word arrived that 120 Brigade was finally in possession of

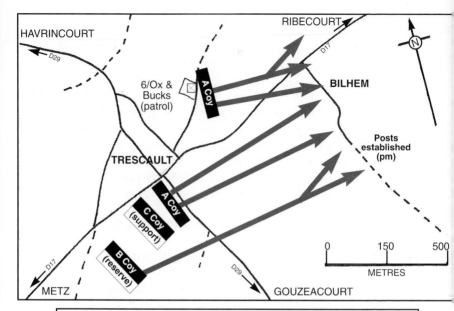

Map 5. 12/KRRC attack on Trescault: 25th April 1917

Beaucamp, patrols were again pushed out. Posts were established on the lane and a significant amount of enemy salvage collected.

In stark contrast to the experience of the Argylls, the attack by the 11/King's Own met with little resistance. By 5.30am patrols were beyond the village and a line well to the east established. Several Argylls wounded the previous day were brought in and sent back to the Field Ambulance. These were joined by a steady trickle of King's Own wounded when the enemy began a slow and methodical bombardment of the newly occupied positions. The war diary reported the battalion's casualties as 'heavy'[12] but actually recorded only seven dead and 61 wounded between 21-25 April. The diarist also noted that the 'spirit of the men throughout the day was excellent'.[13] The battalion's high morale was understandable for, when compared with the Argylls, it had escaped exceptionally lightly; the grim evidence of dozens of crumpled kilted bodies gave testimony to the price paid by the Scots. Having achieved their objective, the Lancastrians were relieved by the 21/Middlesex. German shelling and enemy observation over the new positions meant that connecting up the shell holes into a more substantial line of defence could be attempted only during the hours of darkness.

Two sections of the 231st Field Company and three companies of the divisional Pioneers commenced work digging a communication trench across to the new line. The 13/Yorkshire relieved the 14/HLI in

Villers-Plouich, while further back in Gouzeaucourt, the advanced dressing station of the 136th Field Ambulance was removed from a house to a field on the southern entrance to the village. Here it was protected from enemy fire by a disabled tank. During the battle the transport of the Field Ambulance had proved quite unable to cope with the number of wounded arriving for treatment; fortunately, the evacuation procedure was improved the following day when the ADMS provided the unit with two Ford motor ambulances and additional horse-drawn vehicles.

In 120 Brigade the number of casualties had kept the field ambulances and CCSs to the rear busy. The brigade suffered about five-sixths of the divisional total of 664. The number killed amounted to 133, 107 of whom belonged to 120 Brigade. Of those, 72 came from the Argylls. In addition to its dead the battalion suffered a further seven officers and 153 wounded. The survivors spent the night of 25-26 April bringing in and burying their dead from the fields and ruins of Beaucamp. They were next withdrawn to Etricourt and during 27 April had the maudlin task of sorting the kit of the dead and wounded. The Argylls had suffered more than the other units largely because, with their left flank unprotected, they had been subjected to the severe fire emanating from Bilhem. With an attack on both of its flanks the 13/East Surrey at Villers-Plouich had had an easier task and, according to the divisional history, had enjoyed 'greater support'.[14] The Welsh on Fusilier Ridge had met with so little opposition that the number of killed and wounded was negligible. Similarly, despite the presence of enemy balloons and planes on counter-battery work, the gunners of 181 Brigade RFA had suffered only one man wounded and one damaged limber.

Significant as the capture of Trescault, Bilhem, Beaucamp, Villers-Plouich and Fusilier Ridge were, Fourth Army's task was not yet quite complete. With perhaps predictable insight, the diarist of 12/RB noted: 'It is quite evident that the line we are holding now is going to become a proper system of trenches with communication trenches. The place would be quite a good position except that Havrincourt village looks right down on our positions'.[15] Havrincourt was to remain in German hands for several months but the capture of Bilhem, with its excellent observation over the Hindenburg Line, had necessitated a change in 60 Brigade's defensive scheme. With the assistance of the 83rd Field Company the brigade dug and wired a 3000m long and five feet deep fire trench in only 12 days. All along the front of XV Corps similar activity was undertaken. Communication trenches snaked their way towards the front positions, with strong points, command posts and dug outs constructed at strategic points along their length. There remained, however, one German occupied village between the British and the Hindenburg Line. The 8th and 40th Divisions received orders that La Vacquerie was to be assaulted and captured on 5 May. The attack was timed to be delivered simultaneously with a last effort by the French on the Aisne and only two days after the closure of the major attacks at Arras. Although the assault on La Vacquerie was subsequently downgraded to a large-scale raid, the operation signalled what was to be the last significant attack in the sector for six months.

NOTES

1. F.Whitton, *The History of the 40th Division*, p.60-61
2. Inglefield, op.cit. p.135
3. War diary 181 Bde RFA, op.cit.
4. War diary 12/SWB. WO.95.2606
5. War diary 17/Welch. WO.95.2607
6. Captain Colin Young had been posted to the 17/Welch from the Duke of Wellington's Regiment. He is buried in Fins New British Cemetery.
7. War diary 13/East Surrey. WO.95.2612
8. Ibid
9. Whitton, op.cit. p.70
10. Wandsworth Borough Council has maintained its link, begun in 1920, with the village of Villers-Plouich. British money was used to help rebuild the Mairie, school and to reestablish the water supply. The fireplace in the Mairie records the assistance given by Wandsworth. The 13/East Surrey was originally raised from the Council's various departments. Corporal Foster, who after demobilisation returned to his job at the Town Hall, has been commemorated by a path named in his honour in Wandsworth Park. There is a Villers-Plouich Cup competed for by cricket teams from the council and the local Territorial unit. The Territorials also honour Corporal Foster by an annual dinner.
11. Second Lieutenant Cyril Benson's body was later recovered. He is buried in Neuville-Boujonval Communal Cemetery.
12. War diary 11/King's Own. WO.95.2611
13. Ibid
14. Whitton, op.cit. p.74
15. War diary 12/Rifle Brigade. WO.95.2121

A sap running out of the Hindenburg Line somewhere near Ribécourt.
(IWM Q7845)

Chapter Three

THE RAID ON LA VACQUERIE

The raid on this lonely crest-top village was to be a joint affair between the 8th and 40th Divisions. The purpose, according to the history of the latter division, was to 'inflict loss upon the enemy; to damage his defences and, above all, to obtain identification'. It is a little difficult therefore to understand why the raid had to be conducted on such a large scale. As raids on all sectors of the front usually defined similar if not identical objectives, it is possible that the operation was intended as Rawlinson's finale to the pursuit. By late April he realised that Haig would not sanction an attack on the Hindenburg Line which had as its purpose to breach and hold a section of the defences. A large-scale raid could be justified as an action intended to support the French to the south or as a warning to the enemy that although the Battle of Arras was now officially over, there was to be no respite.

On the 40th Division's front, 119 Brigade was to take the right, with 121 Brigade on the left. The 12/SWB was to attack on the extreme right, with the 17/Welch on its left; the 19/RWF and 18/Welch were to be respectively brigade support and reserve. In 121 Brigade, the 20/Middlesex was on the right and the 12/Suffolk on the left. The objectives of the two brigades were essentially the village of La Vacquerie and the trenches to its north-west. To the south of the 40th Division the 8th was to use the 2/Middlesex and 2/Scottish Rifles of 23 Brigade; one company of the 2/West Yorkshire was also to be involved. Their objectives were the buildings of Sonnet Farm, which lay astride the main Gouzeaucourt-Cambrai road, and Barrack Trench and Support to its south.

Preparations for the raid began in earnest on 29 April. The 12/SWB relieved the 18/Welch in the front line, establishing Battalion HQ in Farnham Quarry beside the railway. Patrols which ventured quite close to La Vacquerie crept about No Man's Land after dark but discovered nothing untoward. The enemy shelled occasionally and aerial activity was reported to be 'above normal'.[1] German patrols seemed not to enter No Man's Land but, behind their lines, they were described as 'being up to their old tricks'[2] of burning farms and other property. With the intention of getting their guns into action by 2 May, on 29 April officers of the 40th TMB had reconnoitred the divisional front. To their

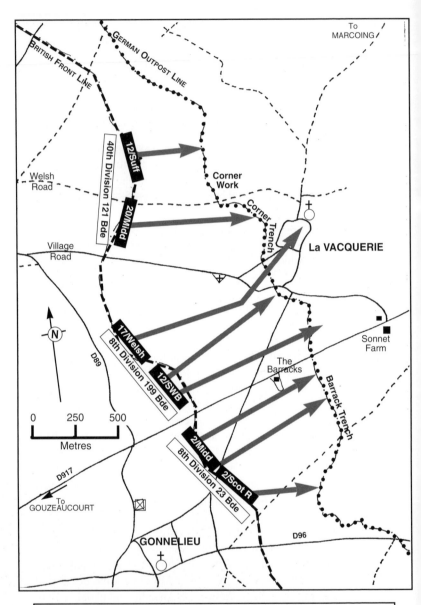

Map 6. The raid on La Vacquerie: 5th May 1917

disappointment, the only possible firing point was discovered to be just behind the British front on the Gouzeaucourt-La Vacquerie road; from this position the village outskirts were at the mortars' extreme range. Furthermore, as the position was not secure from enemy observation, the officers decided that the battery could take no part in the operation. Its gunners spent the next few days in plundering timber and bricks from the ruins of Equancourt to build horse standings and in unloading ammunition for 181 Brigade RFA.

The divisional artillery had meanwhile been zealously engaged in wire-cutting, an activity which had surprisingly drawn only a spasmodic response from the enemy. Despite the reluctance of the German artillery to reply, the frequency with which their front line troops sent up SOS flares suggested that the infantry were certainly nervous about a British attack. Although resultant casualties among the British artillery were light, there were mishaps. Second Lieutenant Sinnet of C/181 Brigade was wounded by a 'prem' fired by C/178 Brigade which, according to one diarist, was 'continually sending prematures into it'.[3] With the intention of testing the enemy's response and discovering where his counter-barrage would fall, batteries were ordered to fire 12 minute trial barrages at 4pm on 4 and 5 May. On both occasions the reply was feeble but the ruse served its purpose. The Germans did however seem to know where the British OPs were sited; they regularly plastered their whereabouts with 4.2-inch shells and the long 77mm shell with instantaneous fuse. This shell gave, in the words of an admiring enemy, 'a remarkably fine detonation'.[4] After dusk

A sergeant inspects a dump of German Bangalore Torpedoes. These explosive pipes were used to destroy wire, obstacles and roads. The village is probably either Metz or Fins.

An officer, armed with walking stick, leads a wiring party along a British communication trench. German belts in front of La Vacquerie and Sonnet Farm were up to 30m thick.

sufficient ammunition was carried up to the batteries to ensure that each gun had over 60 rounds ready for use. Since the decision had been made to alter the operation from an outright assault to a large raid, the guns had each been firing an average of 150 shells per

day against the enemy wire.

The divisional machine-gun companies were also making preparations. In the 40th Division, the 119th and 120th MGC were to cooperate by providing direct overhead fire, while in the 8th Division's sector, eight guns of the 23rd MGC were dug in and camouflaged east and south of Gonnelieu. One hundred thousand rounds were taken up and to save belt-filling during the frenzy of the operation, 42,000 were already in belts. One two gallon tin of water per gun was also in position and night lines were identified by luminous aiming posts. Screens had been made to conceal the guns' flash, two of which had been detailed to go forward with the 2/Scottish Rifles. During the raid the 16 guns of the 119th MGC were eventually to fire off a total of 115,000 rounds.

Signallers of the 40th Division Signal Company had extended telephone cables to the advanced headquarters of artillery and infantry brigades, most of which were sited in or around Gouzeaucourt Wood. On the eastern edge of the wood, orderlies of the 136th Field Ambulance were also making preparations. It had been decided that as the Gouzeaucourt-Cambrai road remained littered with fallen trees, and in the anticipation that Gouzeaucourt itself would be heavily shelled, evacuation of the wounded should be via cross-country tracks. Ambulances would get as far forward as the aid post situated in Fifteen Ravine and would then take the wounded across the fields to Queen's Cross. An ADS was established in the sunken lane between Queen's Cross and Dead Man's Corner, but five dray horses were killed when it came under heavy shell fire on 3 May; two days later the dug out was destroyed. In view of the damage already done, the dressing station was moved during the evening of 5 May to a new position 600m to the south-east.

Zero hour was timed for 11pm on 5 May. Two hours later, as the signal for the raiders to withdraw, platoon commanders in and around La Vacquerie were to strike empty shell cases. Within those two hectic hours the assaulting battalions, mopper-ups, supporting units of sappers, TMB batteries and MGCs were to inflict as much damage as possible. Mobile charges of Stokes bombs to destroy enemy dug outs were carried by sappers of the 224th Field Company and many infantry were issued with 'P' bombs. The raid was intended to be short, sharp and destructive. Its success depended upon whether the wire was cut sufficiently by the artillery, whether the troops could keep direction on a dark, chilly night and, of course, upon the resolution of the German defenders.

When the forward companies advanced at 11pm, those on the left of the attack (121 Brigade) almost immediately ran into difficulty. The 12/Suffolk had its left flank protected by two guns of the 121st TMB; its right flank, where it joined with the 20/Middlesex, lay on Welsh Road 400m west of Corner Trench. D Company of the Suffolk was held up by uncut wire and machine-gun fire and was forced to remain on the receiving end of showers of stick grenades. A Company gained what it thought was its objective, only to realise that they were dummy trenches. In the following confusion one party under Sergeant Lovell became detached and continued on towards the Hindenburg Line. It encountered and despatched an enemy patrol but, having lost touch and unsure of its direction, the group mistakenly continued down Welsh Road towards La Vacquerie. Once inside the village and realising his error, Lovell captured a German sentry and compelled the bewildered man to guide the British back towards their own lines. The group, complete with four prisoners, regained its own lines and Lovell was subsequently awarded an DCM. The bulk of the Suffolk however, having failed to penetrate a second belt of wire in front of Corner Trench, achieved little of any purpose. Besides Lovell's DCM, the only other thing the battalion had to celebrate for the night's work was a MM to Sergeant Jones. Despite heavy shelling, Jones repeatedly repaired a telephone link from Battalion HQ to the front line.

To the right of the Suffolk, Battalion HQ of the 20/Middlesex was established in Farm Ravine. The two assaulting companies were in the ravine by 10.30pm and moved up to fill the line between Welsh and Village Roads. They were in touch with the Suffolk but not with the 17/Welsh of 119 Brigade on their immediate right. At 11.00pm the companies advanced under the barrage, but soon lost three platoon commanders from the German counter-barrage. The troops were pinned down for twenty minutes about 100m west and south-west of a strong point which lay on Welsh Road at the apex of Corner Trench. The surviving officers decided that as it was already 12.30am, even if they could get into the village and beyond Corner Work, there was so little time remaining that the damage they could inflict would be minimal. Consequently the companies withdrew, bringing with them, as ordered, their four dead and 41 wounded.

The two battalions of 121 Brigade had failed in their tasks of entering La Vacquerie and of penetrating down the sunken road towards Marcoing. Their principal problem had been the enormous amount of intact wire. Ten 4.5-inch howitzers and 24 18-pounders had been ordered to blow sufficient gaps in the wire to enable the raiders to get through Corner Trench, Corner Support and Corner Work beyond. On their right, although 119 Brigade had four fewer 4.5-inch howitzers to assist, the SWB and Welch had over double the number of 18-pounders allotted to wire cutting.

Unfortunately, although the guns had done a better job on 119 Brigade's front, there remained a substantial amount of uncut wire. The 17/Welch had moved up from Dessart Wood during the evening of 5 May, rendezvousing successfully with guides from the SWB at the edge of Gouzeaucourt. Major R.J.Andrews, commanding the two attacking companies of the Welch, led his men over in 'excellent order'[5] towards the cross roads south of La Vacquerie. A few casualties were sustained when several British shells fell short and more were added when the Germans awoke to the extent of the danger and opened up with coordinated fire. In spite of some very thick wire and a good deal of opposition, C and A Companies forced their way into the village. Yet more wire was encountered among the cottages but a patrol under Second Lieutenant Waring, using the church tower as a landmark, worked its way down the Marcoing road hoping to gain touch with the Middlesex on its left. Intense fire from the north-west suggested that the Middlesex were not up. Having captured one prisoner, Waring therefore withdrew his patrol and threw out a defensive flank. Numerous enemy flares and rockets lit the dark, leaden sky and many aerial darts plunged around the occupied positions. The Welch hung on while the mopper ups and sappers attended to their nefarious duties.

One company of the 18/Welch was at Farnham Quarry, waiting to advance if called upon to assist the 19/RWF. As mopper-ups the Fusiliers had the task of clearing dug outs and destroying trenches in the village but they had themselves become involved in the actual fighting. Privates Snoddern and Cullen were later awarded the MM for getting into an enemy strong point which the 17/Welch had failed to enter. The sappers too became engaged in close-quarter fighting but did succeed in their primary task of destroying several houses and dug outs. Prisoners of the *459th Regiment* were taken and sent back with the wounded.

At 1am the withdrawal began, B Company of the 17/Welch providing a rearguard on the south-west edge of the village. Each party reported in at the nearby advanced HQ and then B Company and the mopper-ups, bringing with them the wounded, withdrew. The roll was called at Farnham Quarry and by 7am the battalion was back in Dessart Wood.

The right battalion of 119 Brigade was the 12/SWB. Its left company was to attack the extreme southern edge of La Vacquerie, while the right was to enter the trenches between the village and the Cambrai road. The right was soon held up by wire but eventually forced its way through and into Barrier Trench; the left had an easier time until it reached the village. Here again were great swathes of uncut wire. The Borderers dealt with the few enemy they encountered and withdrew according to schedule. One strong patrol was later sent out to bring in two of the dead known to be lying in front of the enemy wire.

Little is known of the part played by the 2/Middlesex. Its exceptionally brief war diary merely records that its two companies were held up near Sonnet Farm and that two officers were wounded. Information regarding the activities of the single company of the 2/West Yorkshire which also took part is similarly difficult to find. Fortunately the 2/Scottish Rifles has left a more substantial account. Its left company apparently lost touch with the Middlesex within ten minutes of the advance commencing. As they lined the eastern banks of two sunken lanes and waited for the barrage to lift, a cold, driving rain beat into the faces of the Cameronians. Patrols two nights earlier had discovered several gaps in the enemy wire but had reported that most of it was intact and substantial. When the companies moved off at zero they made the mistake of striking off at right angles from the sunken lanes which ran diagonally across No Man's Land. This error caused them to lose direction and to come up against yet more uncut wire. Nevertheless, the Rifles did penetrate to the first objective but, even with the arrival of reinforcements, made no progress when attempting to bomb up the enemy trenches. Further efforts were deemed futile so the decision was made to withdraw. With the exception of one party ordered to stay out to bring in any dead and wounded, all companies were back at their start line by 2am.

The Rifles' colonel later reported on what he considered to be the reasons for the failure of this 'unfortunate raid'.[6] He considered the principal causes to be the loss of touch with the Middlesex and the inability to maintain direction once the sunken lanes had been traversed. In addition, a lack of identifiable landmarks, enemy search lights and an insufficient number of gaps in the wire also contributed to the overall failure. New concertina wire had been laid to fill the earlier breaches and the belts over the crest seemed not to have been damaged at all; most of the battalion's 20 dead were thought to have been killed while hung up on the wire. Although orders stressed that no

German dugouts in the Hindenburg Line could be of great depth. Evacuation of wounded from within them often caused problems. RAMC personnel supplemented by German prisoners are using a windlass to haul out a stretcher from such a dugout. The photo was taken during the Battle of Cambrai in the 51st Division's sector.

bodies were to be left in enemy hands, owing to the intensity of the fire, the dead could not be recovered.

So ended this last major action of the pursuit on XV Corps' front. It had proved costly and had achieved very little. Even the normally enthusiastic history of the 40th Division acknowledged that the raid 'fell short probably of expectation'[7], while the historian of the 8th Division 'regretted that it did not meet with better fortune'[8]. All units involved did at least gain some experience in raiding – experience which was to come in handy during the subsequent months. In return for a casualty roll of nearly 200 in 23 Brigade, over 100 in 119 and a similar figure in 121 Brigade, the raid had inflicted only minimal damage on the enemy. If the operation had, as was originally intended, been the capture and holding of La Vacquerie, the cost might well have been justified. In the event, the number of much smaller raids undertaken during the following months achieved as much, if not more, at less expense.

NOTES

1. War diary 12/SWB. op.cit.
2. Ibid
3. War diary 181 Bde RFA. op.cit.
4. Ibid
5. War diary 17/Welch, op.cit.
6. H.Story, *The History of the Cameronians* (Scottish Rifles), p.150
7. Whitton, op.cit. p.79
8. Boraston & Bax, *The Eighth Division in War*, p.117

Chapter Four

LIFE IN THE LINE

Once the dust had settled on the raid at La Vacquerie, British troops in the Villers-Plouich sector adapted to the normal routine of trench warfare. The 8th Division was soon to be withdrawn and although several divisions such as the 9th, 42nd, 48th and 58th did spend time in the area, for the next few months the front between Gonnelieu and Beaucamp was largely in the hands of the 40th Division. It became a 'quiet' sector, where troops at rest could enjoy the summer sun amid relatively comfortable surroundings. There was also work to be done on the defences but, in the rear areas, partridges were sniped for mess suppers and soldiers had the opportunity to spend short leaves in the recovering town of Péronne. Transport for such leave-takers was improved in July when a twice-daily passenger service began on a decauville line between Fins and Péronne. Divisional orders announced that the journey was free, but did warn that the service was likely to be suspended without notice. However, despite the odd comfort, the still very serious business of warfare preoccupied the lives of troops in the line.

The Germans were determined to hold on to the Hindenburg Line and to deny the British any position which might jeopardise its

Metz in 1917. Some four miles behind the front line, the village housed many command posts and brigade headquarters.

security; for the British therefore, it was no longer merely a matter of local engagements against rearguards. At La Vacquerie the 8th and 40th Divisions had received bitter forewarning of the enemy's reaction should the British again have the temerity to attempt a penetration of the Hindenburg Outpost Line. The lesson had also been well learnt at Arras and Bullecourt. Attacks against such defences required tactics different to frontal infantry assaults supported by penny packets of tanks. For now the 40th Division was content to hold the line and conduct raids against the foremost enemy positions.[1] The Germans were not of course happy to sit idly by. They answered the British raids with those of their own and were only too willing to plaster the front and rear with salvos of howitzer shells and minnewerfers. 'Quiet' it may have been in comparative terms to Messines and Ypres, but a sinecure it was not.

For those in the line there was the usual boredom of trench holding and maintenance, interspersed by sometimes hours of terror during regular periods of 'hate'. The normal routine was four days in the front trenches, four in support, four in reserve and four at rest. A steady if undramatic drain went on throughout the tours; intermittent shelling, patrolling and snipers all took their toll and gradually the cemeteries at Villers-Plouich, Beaucamp and Gouzeaucourt expanded in area to accommodate the increasing number of wooden crosses. When out of the line, troops were engaged in a multitude of activities: assisting the

Officers had a responsibility to check the condition of their men's feet. In an example of a text book trench a RAMC officer examines feet for signs of trench foot.

Communications in the forward areas were always difficult. Air lines suspended on short poles were used behind the lines to link brigade, division and corps headquarters.

RE to construct horse standings, supplying carrying parties from the light railways to brigade or battalion dumps, providing labour for the Tunnelling Companies mining in Fifteen Ravine, digging and wiring reserve positions, moving guns and improving the camps around Dessart Wood. In some battalions all companies provided permanent sanitary parties of 20 men and Pioneer sections of a similar number. Engineers of the Divisional Signal Company laid and suspended miles of cables to Queen's Cross and to the several brigade HQ centred near Dessart and Gouzeaucourt Woods.

Trench maintenance made constant demands upon the troops. Revetting, trench boarding, digging sumps and extending saps were done during the hours of darkness and, when local conditions permitted, in daylight. In occasional surges of unexpected violence the elements could destroy much of the work done by the sweat and labour of the RE, infantry and gunners. On 14 May a particularly wild storm erupted upon the trenches in the Trescault and Villers-Plouich sectors. The HQ dug out of the 14/Argyll & Sutherland Highlanders and the nearby shelters sited in a quarry on the Gouzeaucourt-Villers-Guislain road were submerged in a tidal wave of flood water. A similar fate befell 60 Brigade's HQ near Trescault. In the trenches themselves the HQ of 12/KRRC at Dead Man's Corner was flooded to a depth of six feet. The Orderly Room was awash with papers and filthy water, but with the assistance of pumps and a great deal of hard work, propriety was eventually restored. Another storm in June again reduced the sunken lanes to torrents of foaming water and the ravines to impassable bogs. A legacy of this last storm was a plague of frogs. So many hundreds of the creatures took up residency in the front trenches held by the 13/Yorkshire that scores were massacred by men tramping up and down the duckboards. As the mushrooming number of squashed bodies developed into a potential health hazard, a number of

The winter of 1917-18 was very severe. Troops improvised means of keeping their feet warm and dry. These men have wrapped sand bags around their boots.

Green Howards were appointed battalion frog catchers. Any captured creatures were placed in sandbags and delivered daily to Battalion HQ. The rain also kept sappers of the 231st Field Company busy. Parties spent much of July draining the burgeoning site of Tyke Dump, a little to the south-west of Gouzeaucourt, and on improving the sumps along Leicester Avenue near Beaucamp. In preparation for winter the company constructed a gumboot store at the northern end of Villers-Plouich.

There were too, of course, lighter moments: Etricourt was often the scene of battalion sports days, parties of ten men left weekly on leave and the rare draft might offer the opportunity to renew disrupted friendships. In 119 Brigade for example, seven of a draft of 51 to the 12/SWB and 15 of 57 to the 18/Welch had previously served with their new found battalions. The 12/Suffolk in 121 Brigade did even better. Of a draft of 42 men, 18 had previously served with the unit. In late June the 13/Yorkshire mustered for a swimming parade, the first enjoyed by the battalion since its arrival in France 12 months earlier. The opportunity was apparently 'greatly appreciated by all ranks'.[2] Medal parades to honour those who had shown outstanding bravery were usually held at Etricourt or Equancourt and provided the chance to knock a little rust off ceremonial skills.

One feature of life in the Villers-Plouich sector was the amount of aerial activity. War diaries frequently note the regularity of dog fights

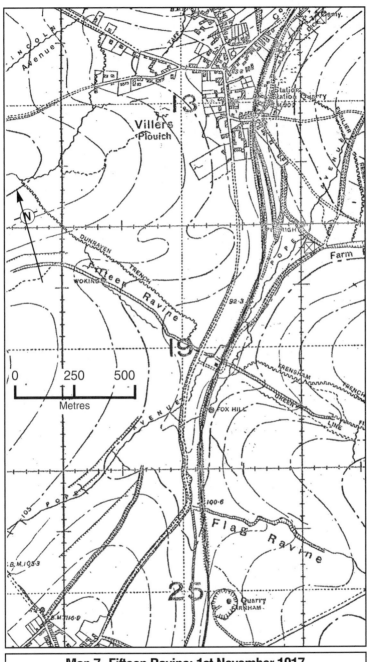

Map 7. Fifteen Ravine: 1st November 1917

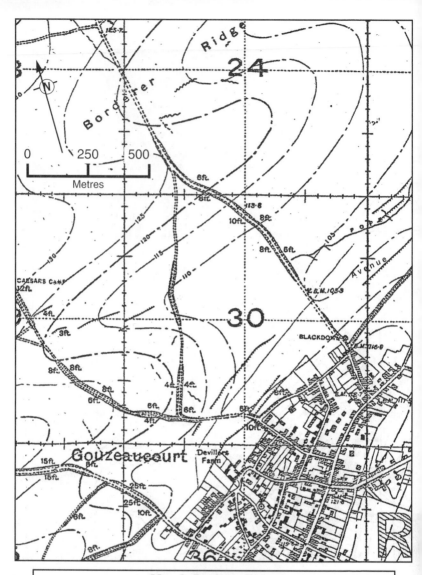

Map 8. Borderer Ridge

and the number of observation balloons floating above the trenches. During training periods battalions did sometimes spend some time working with contact aircraft, and officers of 181 Brigade RFA combined sight-seeing trips and observation duties with a balloon company operating from Heudicourt. During a misty early morning in May, troops of the 19/RWF were instructed to fire off five dozen Very lights for the benefit of observers belonging to the 16th Balloon

Company. In July the 12/SWB brought down an enemy plane by rifle and Lewis-gun fire and, having watched a British plane crash in flames near Metz, soldiers of the 14/Argyll & Sutherland Highlanders opened up with everything they possessed when the victorious enemy crossed their lines. Despite the combined massed fire of rifles and Lewis guns, the German pilot and plane cruised on unmolested. A few days later the battalion watched as a Sopwith Scout was jumped by a horde of enemy aircraft above Beaucamp. The pilot, Second Lieutenant Cole, managed to land his damaged craft just behind the lines and was whisked away to a field ambulance with a bullet in his thigh. On the same day a little to the north, riflemen of 12/KRRC saw another British plane crash near Gouzeaucourt and two British observers bale out of their balloon when it was attacked by enemy scouts. In October, Private Handley of the 13/Yorkshire was awarded the MM for helping the pilot and observer get clear from their crashed machine 500 yards behind the lines.

During the short summer nights troops in the front line sometimes amused themselves by pinning newspapers onto the enemy wire. In response to having discovered copies of the German-produced *Les Ardennes Gazette* on their own wire, a patrol of the 12/SWB attached some official British releases to the enemy wire the following night. The 14/Argyll & Sutherland Highlanders and the 18/Welch fired facsimiles of letters, purportedly written by German prisoners of war, from Stokes mortars and undetonated rifle grenades into German trenches near La Vacquerie. Risks for no real gain were frequently

Signallers would cross No Man's Land with the early waves of assaulting troops to establish signal stations or report centres. Electric flash lamps could be used when local conditions allowed.

Some methods of obtaining water at the front – including melted snow.

attempted. For example, during the darkness of 20-21 July, Second Lieutenant J.W.Wilson and 20 men of the 13/East Surrey crept from a sap near Welsh Trench and crawled across No Man's Land. Their quarry was a large notice board hung on the enemy wire in front of Corner Trench. As soon as the party began to cut the wire a light was played on the board from the German trenches and two machine guns opened a cross fire. Two of the Surrey were wounded as they dived for whatever cover the ground could provide. During the course of the next 90 minutes the patrol tried to grab the board three times; on each occasion enemy fire erupted around them. Eventually Wilson signalled the withdrawal and the raiders returned. For his part in the affair, the subaltern was awarded the MC.

Active, assertive patrolling soon became a doctrine for the 40th Division. In the nights following the raid on La Vacquerie and throughout the remainder of the summer and early autumn, small groups of officers and men crawled across No Man's Land to investigate the enemy's wire and listening posts. The information they collected was often used in the planning of large raids. The job was dangerous and, at times, deadly. Second Lieutenant Trevor Mills of the 13/East Surrey ordered his patrol to remain outside the German wire as he went further on towards Banteux. The patrol heard firing and Mills did not return.[3] Six days later Major G.Atkinson and five men of the 21/Middlesex were somewhat luckier. Having lost direction, the party spent 50 hours in No Man's Land until Lewis-gun fire finally convinced them of the position of the British trenches. In July the 12/SWB lost Second Lieutenant Snelson killed and seven wounded when they encountered an enemy patrol in No Man's Land and the 17/Welch lost four men when a patrol failed to return. A small party went out the following night but failed to discover any trace of the men.

From time to time the enemy was seen in daylight. From their positions on the northern slope of Welsh Ridge, British observers could see German train movements in and out of Cambrai and even in the front lines the enemy occasionally took liberties which would not have been considered in a more active area. In May, sentries of the 13/East Surrey saw two Germans, later identified as belonging to the *162nd Regiment*, walking about in front of the British wire near Beaucamp; the two were sniped and at night their bodies were recovered. In more adventurous manner Lance Corporal Rogers of the 17/Welch received the MM for capturing an enemy signaller in No Man's Land. The unfortunate German was seen looking confused and lost in front of the British wire on Cemetery Ridge. Rogers crept out,

Winchester Valley, east of Metz. During the Cambrai offensive a British naval gun fired from the siding which ran along the valley. Light railways connected with the broad gauge and ran through Gouzeaucourt Wood.

stalked him through the long grass and brought him back for interrogation.

In the absence of any really major offensive the divisional artillery suffered a reduction in its daily allocation of shells. In May the number of shells per 18-pounder battery of 181 Brigade RFA was increased to 246 rounds – half being HE and half shrapnel; the 4.5-inch howitzer batteries were each allowed 125 rounds. In June the ammunition allotment was slashed to 42 rounds for the 18-pounders and 30 for the howitzers. It probably raised the gunners' hackles when some of this limited supply was misspent. For example, 178 Brigade RFA blazed away for 20 minutes in response to what it thought was an SOS from the front line. It later transpired that the two observed rockets had in fact been fired from the German lines. The reduction in allocation is reflected in the number of shells handled by the Divisional Ammunition Column. In May a total of 65,443 shells, of which 9934 were 4.5-inch, were issued to the divisional batteries. By August the total had fallen to 16,307 and in September only 9856, 2120 of which were howitzer shells, were distributed. The MGCs too had many what they called 'quiet nights'.[4] Even these, however, could easily involve the expenditure of 5000 rounds. When they fired concentration shoots at German rear areas, the number of rounds rose significantly. For example, a fairly minor barrage on Good Man Farm by the 119th MGC used 10,000 rounds and, when assisting a raid by the HLI in September, the 22 Vickers of the 224th MGC fired off over 101,000 rounds. In a fairly typical month which might have included a few feint barrages and some daylight sniping but no direct assistance to an infantry raid, one company could use 150,000 bullets.

The divisional batteries and MGCs could also be on the receiving end of enemy retaliation. One intense strafe on 181 Brigade RFA

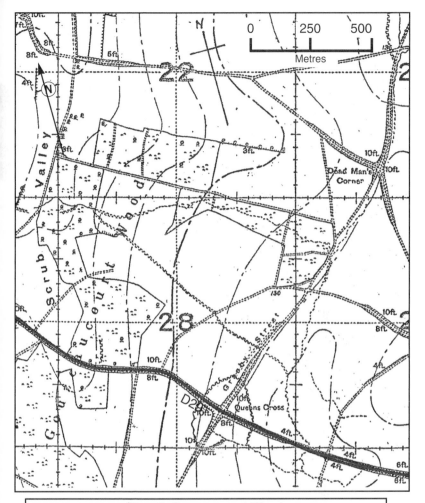

Map 9. Gouzeaucourt Wood

positions was followed by another, equally furious, one day later. The battery's guns were in a crowded area near Gouzeaucourt Wood and, having sustained several casualties, were put out of action for nearly 24 hours. By the end of July, 181 Brigade was up to strength in men and animals, over strength in officers, yet seven guns short of establishment. In addition to working the guns the crews had been heavily engaged in strengthening gun pits and observation posts throughout the month. Each observation post had been provided with a mined dug out and it was intended that every 18-pounder battery position should have such a shelter, with a cupola supported by iron rails and reinforced concrete above the guns. The howitzers were to rely on camouflage for protection.

Dug outs offered some protection from HE, but provided little comfort during a gas barrage. Both sides used gas fairly liberally during the summer and four stretcher bearers of the 17/Welch were awarded the MM for entering a heavily drenched area and bringing out wounded comrades. The gassed and wounded were evacuated to one of three divisional field ambulances positioned behind the front.

The most recent of the arrival of the three was the 135th Field Ambulance. Having moved forward from Maricourt to Fins, it took over the divisional main dressing station and divisional baths from the 136th Field Ambulance. It also assumed responsibility for an advanced dressing station at Caesar's Camp and for two bearer posts at Fifteen Ravine and the sunken lane west of Villers-Plouich. The ADS, which usually carried a staff of one officer and 16 orderlies, could accommodate eight lying cases and was generally about 1500m from regimental aid posts. There was one ADS for each of the two brigades in the line. Each of the brigades had a local loading point for the Decauville railway link to the casualty clearing stations at Ytres and Fins: that for the left brigade was in Scrub Valley immediately west of Gouzeaucourt Wood, while that for the right was in the fields south-west of Gouzeaucourt not far from Tyke Dump.

Since April 1917 the 137th Field Ambulance had dealt with the sick of those units in the 40th Division which did not have a Regimental Medical Officer and details of those whose MO was in the line. The average number of daily patients in May was 120; they suffered from a variety of complaints ranging from boils and blisters to ulcers. Sick cases which were adjudged likely to recover quickly were detained in its two wards which could accommodate 75 patients. These were housed in former stables close to the unit's two operating tents. Cases which required more prolonged treatment were sent to XV Corps MDS at Fins or direct to Péronne. During a two week period in June the approximately 100 staff of the field ambulance admitted four officers and 276 other ranks (including one escaped Russian prisoner of war) and treated 2028 sick and slightly wounded.

Largely because it was considered to be a quiet area, the strength of some battalions in the division tended to be well below establishment. In August the 19/RWF was down to 452 all ranks and in late September the 13/East Surrey could muster only 19 officers and 480 other ranks. By contrast, the July strength of the 12/Suffolk was an astonishing 38 officers and 864 men. The total of all ranks in the 11/King's Own is unknown but in late September the battalion received a massive draft

During periods of static warfare light railways were of crucial importance in lightening some of the burden of the infantry. Depending upon the lie of the land, the tracks could sometimes extend to the support trenches. Stores, rations and troops could be brought up and the wounded evacuated.

of 240. This seems somewhat excessive because its casualties for the entire month amounted to only one killed and ten wounded. It could be that the battalion had been so reduced and had received perhaps no drafts at all since March that such an influx was considered to be a necessity. However, as the strength of several other battalions also increased during September, the pessimists no doubt predicted a move to a more active area.

In addition to the scores of patrols that weekly slipped over the bags to prowl around the expanse of No Man's Land, the 40th Division undertook a staggering number of raids against the enemy defences. Many involved perhaps 30 men while others could employ upwards of one company. The 17/Welch was the first battalion to try its hand, choosing to investigate the Barracks and a trench south-east of La Vacquerie. Following a five minute barrage, three officers and 30 men divided into three parties, dashed through gaps in the wire and bombed towards each other up and down the enemy trench. They captured two men of the *82nd Reserve Regiment* and discovered the Barracks to be empty. There were no casualties and 'all arrangements worked admirably'.[5] The success of the enterprise was put down to the 'dash and discipline of the men engaged who obeyed their instructions to the letter'.[6] The diarist of 181 Brigade RFA, which had fired the covering barrage, recorded simply, 'the enemy went on their knees and squealed'.[7]

Two other very successful raids were made by the 14/HLI in September and the 18/Welch in early October. In preparation for the HLI's attempt on Farm Trench the artillery blew two feint gaps in the enemy wire and shrouded Highland Ridge in smoke. Nine sappers of the 231st Field Company were to accompany the HLI and the 224th MGC cooperated with 22 Vickers firing along directed lines. A few minutes before zero a number of dummies worked by wire made a demonstration further down the British line. A later report suggested that although it was 'doubtful if they drew fire', they 'did undoubtedly contribute to deceiving the enemy'.[8] Carrying smoke candles and 'P' bombs, the HLI swept across No Man's Land and into Farm Trench. While raiders and most of the the sappers hurled Stokes bombs into dug outs and put Bangalore torpedoes down others, one party of RE blew return gaps through the wire. For a cost of four dead and 19 wounded, the raiders estimated that they had killed 60 Germans and returned with ten prisoners. In preparation for its raid against an enemy redoubt on Welsh Road, the 18/Welch had sent out three reconnoitring patrols and had had the four officers and 60 men to be involved training hard for their task at Nurlu. Covered by a fighting patrol and accompanied by eight sappers, the Welsh killed a number of Germans, brought one back and destroyed two dug outs.

Given the number of raids and patrols creeping about No Man's Land, it is not surprising that sometimes rival parties stumbled across each other. On one such occasion a patrol of the 12/SWB under the command of Second Lieutenant Williams lost one man killed but despatched five Germans who were approaching the British wire. Williams was awarded the MC and Private Creighton the MM.

No matter how hard the raiders trained and how thorough the preparations, things could, and frequently did, go wrong. Four days after its first successful raid the 17/Welch attempted another. At 1.55am on 22 May, two officers and 30 men lined up 100 yards north of the Cambrai road. The intention was to raid the enemy trenches south of La Vacquerie and if possible penetrate as far as Sonnet Farm. Unfortunately, the barrage lasted longer than scheduled and several of the party were wounded even before they reached the German wire. Several machine guns opened up and in the intense darkness, driving rain and with one third of the raiders already knocked over, it was

Map 10. Villers-Plouich: 20th November 1917

decided to abandoned the attempt. Covered by a patrol in front of the British wire and bringing with them their ten wounded, the raiders were back in their own trenches by 3.15am. In June the battalion tried twice again and met with no more success on either occasion. On 18 June, Captain Stratton led 42 men towards Farm Trench but they were forced to withdraw when the fuses of both Bangalore torpedoes failed to explode. They tried again the following night, bringing with them on this occasion Lance Corporal Mellors of the 224th Field Company to fire the Bangalore. When they were within 20 yards of the enemy wire, heavy fire forced them to withdraw. Two men were killed and six wounded, but Lieutenant Elmitt, who 'set an example of coolness and contempt for danger beyond all praise'[9], and Second Lieutenant Griffiths were awarded the MC. Private Henry Holman, whose gallantry in organising parties to carry back the wounded was 'extraordinary'[10], was given the DCM. Undeterred by these setbacks, in July the battalion made two further attempts towards Farm Trench. On the first try the party was attacked in No Man's Land by four enemy patrols and on the second the Bangalore again failed to explode. The 44 raiders tried to hack their way through the wire by hand but the belts were too thick and they eventually withdrew.

Barrack Trench, south of the Cambrai road, was the objective of several raids in August by the 12/SWB. On one occasion two officers and 61 other ranks passed through a gap in the wire blown by sappers and bombed up the trench for 100 yards. The enemy brought down a bombardment on his own trench and, amid the confusion, a German flare was misinterpreted by the raiders as the signal to withdraw. With two dead and 10 wounded the Borderers retired to their own lines on Cemetery Ridge. In September over 100 all ranks of the 19/RWF raided Barrack and Barrier Trenches, north and south of the Cambrai road. Thick belts of wire hampered progress and the signal to withdraw was given before either of the trenches had been entered. The battalion was awarded three MCs and ten MMs for the three raids it undertook in the space of a two week period.

The 17/Welch was again active during August and, once again, things did not go according to plan. On two successive nights, Captain Higson and Second Lieutenant Borrie RE led 30 men against Farm Trench and, on both attempts, the wire proved too thick; one Bangalore blew the first belt but not a second 30 yards behind. Higson attempted to cut his way through but was mortally wounded while still working on the first belt. His body, and that of another man killed alongside him, was brought back when the raid was abandoned.[11] A combined effort on Bleak Walk, Barrack Trench and Barrack Support by the 18/Welch and 12/SWB on 4 July coincided with a German raid on the Argylls' trenches on Welsh Ridge. The noise of fitting up Bangalores beneath the German wire was partly disguised by deliberate bursts of machine-gun fire but, once again, the thickness of successive belts of wire thwarted the attempts of 119 Brigade to reach its objective. German shelling on the British wire a little to the north had meanwhile created two gaps. The Argylls positioned extra Lewis guns to cover the breaches; fortunately for their crews, a later shower of German stick grenades fell short of these posts. The Lewis guns opened up and the enemy fled back to Corner Trench. Less than three weeks later the Argylls were again on the receiving end of a German raid. An enemy party entered an unoccupied section of Mountain Ash Trench lying between Surrey Road and the Villers-Plouich-Marcoing road and was only forced out after a severe bombing engagement. Although wounded himself, CSM Snowden guarded Lieutenant Landell's mortally wounded body until the Germans had been ejected.[12]

The Germans too could run into difficulties when raiding. An alert sentry of the 13/East Surrey in a saphead on Welsh Road raised the alarm when an estimated 30 Germans approached his position.

A pile of German helmets taken from German prisoners during the Cambrai offensive.

Grenades were exchanged and for some minutes sounds of groaning were heard in No Man's Land. Two NCOs of the *123rd Grenadiers* were captured when a raid went wrong against some British trenches on Cemetery Ridge and two abandoned Bangalores and over 500 grenades and rifles were recovered by the 17/Welch near Surrey Road.

The most stunning success of the summer's nocturnal activity was enjoyed by the Germans at the expense of the 13/Yorkshire. Early warning of the intended raid was provided by a German deserter so, when an intense box barrage smashed down on the Howards' trenches on Highland Ridge, the divisional artillery immediately responded. Nevertheless, the Germans fought their way into the British positions, killing five and wounding six before making off with the incredible number of 25 prisoners. The divisional history attempted to play down

The line of electricity poles heads towards the site of the Monument above Villers-Plouich. The lone tree (left) is on the route of Surrey Road. The photo is taken from the D56, about 1000m behind the German outpost line and looks towards the position of Farm Trench. This area was the scene of several raids during the summer of 1917.

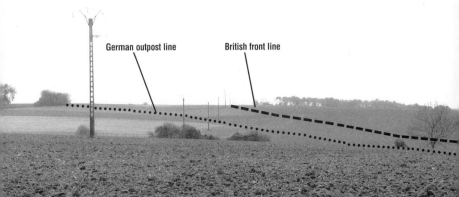

the degree of success, claiming that 'the battalion, after the first surprise, got down to it with great resolution and deprived the Germans of the greater success for which they had probably hoped'.[13] It is somewhat difficult to imagine for what more the Germans could possibly have hoped.

The biggest effort of the summer was undoubtedly that undertaken by the 12/Suffolk in late September. Six parties, totalling eight officers and 236 men, raided Quarry Trench. This was a continuation of Bleak Trench and ran parallel to and just south of the Gonnelieu-Banteux road. Dummies were again employed to deceive the enemy and under cover of smoke the Suffolk went across carrying thermite bombs. Unfortunately, they were caught by the German barrage as they crossed No Man's Land and as they picked their way through the wire. Although they gained a bag of five prisoners, the raiders suffered severely; nearly 50% of those who took part became casualties. Nevertheless, the 13/Yorkshire, who relieved the Suffolk the next night, believed the raid had achieved a 'quieting effect on the enemy. His machine-gun fire greatly diminished and his activity generally during the early stages of this tour was at a minimum'.[14]

One of the most frequently stated reasons for conducting a raid was the desire to maintain unit morale. There are many examples where successful raids did apparently improve esprit but, given the comparative quiet of the 40th Division's sector, morale does not seem to have been a particular worry to the authorities. There was at least one man in the division, however, whose morale did take something of a battering during the month of July. Captain Norman Reid was the CO of the Divisional TMB. Frustrated at having been unable to take part in the raid on La Vacquerie, Reid finally managed to get his guns into action at Gonnelieu on 14 May. In retaliation for the unit's first hostile bombs, Reid's observation post was demolished by a salvo of 5.9-inch shells. He blamed the accuracy of the German shells on 'the infantry and other people wandering in at all hours of the day in full view of the German trenches'.[15] That same evening a detachment arrived at the guns bringing with it three rounds. The carrying party found the guns but could not locate their crews. To make matters worse, during a bombardment the following day, enemy shrapnel ruined several of Reid's precious bombs.

Despite having established a new OP, 16 May brought little satisfaction to Reid. Enemy aircraft and balloons soared over the ruins of Gonnelieu and, to add to the misery, it was discovered that eight of the mortars' charges were soaking wet and useless. Following an angry

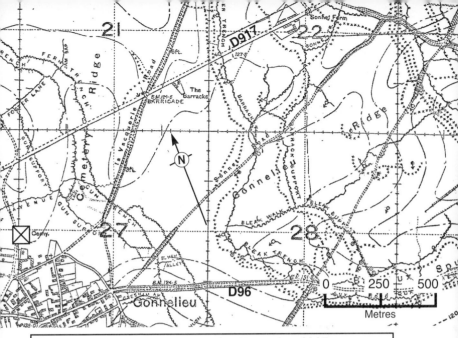

Map 10. Gonnelieu: 20th November 1917

exchange with the personnel at the bomb store, who refused to provide replacement charges for those ruined by the damp, ten more bombs were eventually brought up.

Things improved a little the following day. After an exhaustive search, Reid decided upon a new position for the guns. He sited them in the yard of a ruined house in Gonnelieu, the surviving brickwork of which hid them from enemy view. Furthermore, the yard possessed two deep former German dug outs; one was used to accommodate the crews and the other was quickly requisitioned as a bomb store. The disadvantage of the new site was that only one short part of the German defences could be observed from it. The guns nevertheless fired an average of five bombs each day at this single target. Not surprisingly, the Germans became irritated at this concentration on one part of their line and retaliated. So heavy was the enemy response that the CO of the Argylls requested that Reid's mortars should be used only for retaliating to German initiatives. It was his men in the trenches, rather than the mortar crews themselves, who tended to suffer when the Germans answered. Reid rather testily recorded that unlike the Argylls: 'The King's Own did not seem to notice or mind retaliation'.[16] Three days later the CO of the King's Own confounded Reid's assumption when he too petitioned the battery not to fire for 24 hours. This pause would, he explained, provide the time necessary for one of his companies to change the position of its HQ. Its existing site had been repeatedly bracketed by German shells searching for the mortars. Reid insisted that the enemy guns were only attracted to his position because 'infantry and other people will persist in wandering down the road under observation and then walking into our gun position out of curiosity'.[17] Things went from bad to worse on 6 June when a 4.2-inch shell landed squarely in the bomb store. The mortars themselves were unharmed and fired off a salvo in retaliation. The shock of the guns, however, released clouds of brick dust from the largely demolished store. These hung suspiciously above the battery position for five minutes. Watching Germans assumed the clouds told a story and again plastered the site with shells of various calibres.

In a diary entry of early July, Reid allowed his pent-up frustration to boil over. Instead of hitting a German communication trench called Bleak Walk, the CO of the 18/Welch accused the mortars of dropping

A 60cm light railway track winding its way across the devastated zone. In November 1917 it was intended to link the German track at La Vacquerie with the extended British one running from Gouzeaucourt within two days.

A variety of visual methods was used to pass messages between forward and supporting troops. Here, two signallers are using Morse code and a shutter to relay information.

22 rounds into his own front trench. It was, thundered Reid:

> Partly through crass ignorance and partly through deliberate false statements that this absurd report was sent in. CRA (Brigadier-General Nicholson) with the assistance of aerial photos taken on 6 July easily routed the opposition. It is obvious that most of the infantry are extraordinarily ignorant and criminally unobservant, or that they will go to any length to prevent our firing because infantry officers observing from our front lines from which every portion of hostile line is totally invisible, send in fatuous reports about our bombs falling in or near our wire when in fact they have fallen 700 yards away!! This happens nearly every day and is extremely annoying and unfair. A cursory glance at any aerial photo of Bleak Walk and vicinity and our line would convince them of their error. Instead of getting the support of our infantry we meet with opposition. The Battery was congratulated by the Divisional Commander on its excellent shooting and destruction of Bleak Walk and Bleak Trench, and we're told not to fire for a few days as the targets had been destroyed.[18]

The divisional commander's mellifluous words were probably a concession to his disgruntled infantry and an acknowledgement that a heavy-mortar battery could sometimes do as much harm as good. The General's caution was justified for, when two weeks later the battery again received permission to fire, the eight rounds it landed on Bleak Walk drew such overwhelming retaliation from German howitzers that not only was the battery position smashed but the ruins of Gonnelieu were pummelled into yet smaller fragments. Relations between Reid and the CO of the 17/Welch in particular remained caustic for the remainder of the division's stay in the sector.

Reid's battery was to remain in the sector for some two weeks after the bulk of the division had withdrawn to rest. Another unit which also stayed working in the area after the division had left was the Pioneer battalion, the 12/Yorkshire. The Teeside Pioneers spent most of their time in the Villers-Plouich area providing what their chronicler described as 'housemaid parties'. Such groups were normally engaged in general trench maintenance. Digging, wiring and revetting were the most usual tasks but their engineering skills were often put to more specialist work. Casualties were never severe but the unit underwent a massive alteration in its character and personnel in September when it was ordered to exchange 369 of its own men for an identical number of Royal Engineers. The Pioneers were finally withdrawn from the sector some ten days after the division had gone, handing over their camp, shelters and work to their colleagues of the 11/DLI, Pioneers to the 20th Division.

In October the 20th Division made its reappearance in the Villers-Plouich sector. In May it had relinquished its positions around Havrincourt Wood and Trescault to the Lancashire Territorials of the 42nd Division. The 42nd, only recently arrived from Egypt, had already raised the ire of the 48th Division in the nearby Epéhy area. The Midlanders blamed the loss of the strategically important position of Gillemont Farm on the poor performance of battalions of the Manchester Regiment. The Lancastrians, who had been in Egypt and Gallipoli since September 1914, soon also upset the 40th Division. Following a temporary redistribution of brigade fronts, the 21/Middlesex relieved the 8/Lancashire Fusiliers at Villers-Plouich. Three hours after a difficult relief was finally completed, a German barrage isolated a forward post held by the Middlesex. An enemy squad descended upon the post, capturing the unfortunate Private Dickenson and a Lewis gun. After making enquiries of the departed Fusiliers, the Middlesex blamed them for the loss of Dickenson. The Lancastrians had apparently not undertaken a single patrol during the previous week and had not realised that the wire protecting Dickenson's post had been cut some time before the raid took place.

The 20th Division did not yet know the purpose behind its return to the sector and, for the time being, busied itself with preparing for the onset of winter. When the 6/Ox & Bucks relieved the 14/HLI at Villers-

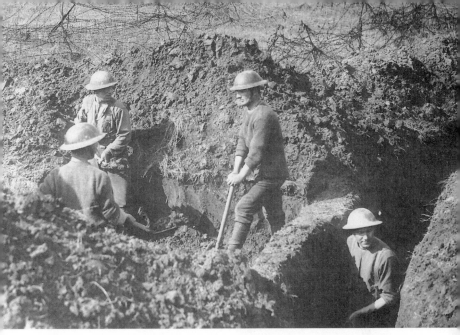

Telephone cables from brigade headquarters to the forward positions were buried as deeply as possible. This working party is digging a cable trench at Metz shortly before the German offensive. (IWM Q855)

Plouich its Intelligence Officer remarked that the enemy was 'practically inactive'.[19] An exceptionally chatty diarist of 12/RB concurred with his colleague's sentiments. He noted that: 'To relieve in the day time is a great change. All the companies have good accommodation and in many places the men have beds...The whole place seems absurdly quiet and comfortable to what we have been experiencing up North'.[20] The 12/KRRC thought the trenches it took over from the 11/King's Own at Beaucamp were 'very good indeed', but did consider that the front line was deficient in shelters and that a 'good deal of revetting will be necessary before winter really cuts in'.[21]

The general defensive system employed by the 40th Division in early autumn consisted of scattered, unconnected platoon posts in the front line. The intervening gaps were patrolled night and day by two men. The 20th Division decided that as these intervals provided good cover for enemy snipers, several further posts should be constructed. This work was commenced in mid-October but was hampered by a shortage of RE material. In early November the system was again altered. In front of Beaucamp for example, one battalion of 60 Brigade concentrated its efforts on establishing two defended localities on Highland Ridge. The left boundary was a communication trench called Oxford Lane, running parallel to and on the southern side of Lancaster

Two men of the 36th Division in the village of Metz sometime in 1917.
IWM Q6092

Map 12. Trescault: 20th November 1917

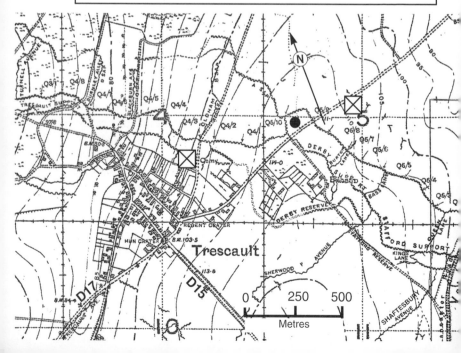

Road; the right boundary was another communication trench called Grantham Avenue, roughly equidistant from Argyle Road and the main Villers-Plouich-Ribécourt road. The old support line 600m east of Beaucamp now became the main line of resistance; the former front line was then held as an outpost line of Lewis guns manned by two companies of four posts each. A battalion and RE dump in Beaucamp was replenished nightly by a convoy of motor lorries which could get as far as Charing Cross in comparative safety.

The more relaxed warfare experienced by the 20th Division in its new location also provided a triumph for 12/RB. In jubilation its chronicler recorded 'at last, a Boche prisoner'.[22] The man in question was 'found walking along our trench on D Company's front'. Although the battalion claimed him as a capture, the diarist had the honesty to note that 'evidently he had meant to give himself up having deserted from a patrol'.[23]

A scene repeated many times following the German withdrawal. French civilians returned to their former cottages to dig for their buried valuables. In 1917 troops of the 42nd Division in the Trescault area spent frantic days digging up gardens after a French civilian had recovered a hoard of gold coin.

While the men of the 20th Division might have been anticipating something of a rest following their labours at Ypres, those of the 40th were perhaps showing signs of anxiety. They had been in the line almost continually for six months, battalions were being brought closer to establishment and there had been a progressive programme of training for those units not in the forward positions. The division was expecting a rest but could not anticipate another such cushy posting. It concentrated first at Fosseux and then at Lucheux. The countryside there contained thickly wooded hills and valleys. The three infantry brigades were to spend two weeks training in wood fighting - skills which were to prove useful in late November when they struggled among the gas and blood-soaked stumps of Bourlon Wood.

NOTES

1. Rawlinson had perhaps not completely abandoned hopes of launching a major attack as on 6 June 1917 the CRA 40th Division told his officers that an offensive against La Vacquerie, involving an additional twelve field artillery brigades, was in the planning stage.
2. War diary 13/Yorkshire. op.cit.
3. Second Lieutenant Mills is commemorated on the Thiepval memorial.
4. War diary 119th MGC. WO.95.2607
5. War diary 17/Welch. op.cit.
6. Ibid
7. War diary 181st Bde RFA. op.cit.
8. War diary 231st Field Coy.RE. WO.95.2601
9. War diary 17/Welch. op.cit.
10. Ibid
11. Captain Frederick Higson is buried in Gouzeaucourt New British Cemetery.
12. Lieutenant William Landell is buried in Rocquigny-Equancourt Road British Cemetery.
13. Whitton, op.cit. p.82
14. War diary 13/Yorkshire. op.cit.
15. War diary 40th Division TMB. WO.95.2599
16. Ibid
17. Ibid
18. Ibid
19. War diary 6/Ox & Bucks. WO.95.2120
20. War diary 12/Rifle Brigade. WO.95.2121
21. War diary 12/KRRC. WO.95.2120
22. War diary 12/Rifle Brigade. op.cit.
23. Ibid

Taken on 10 December 1917, the old British front line near Trescault.

(IWM Q7842)

Chapter Five

THE BATTLE OF CAMBRAI

A readjustment of Army and Corps boundaries during the summer meant that when the 20th Division moved into the Villers-Plouich sector it became part of III Corps, Third Army. It was to be joined a few weeks later in the line by the 6th and 12th Divisions. Together with the 29th Division, which became corps reserve, these four divisions constituted III Corps for the majority of the Battle of Cambrai. The Corps' boundary stretched from Banteux Ravine in the south to Beaucamp Valley in the north. The village of Trescault and the adjoining area of Bilhem lay in IV Corps' sector and will be mentioned only briefly in the following narrative.

The genesis for an attack against the Havrincourt-Flesquières Ridge had appeared in May but the subsequent offensives at Messines and Ypres took priority and, as we have seen, III Corps at Villers-Plouich had a relatively peaceful time. Further plans were submitted during the summer but the projected offensive remained in abeyance until mid-September when Haig again turned his thoughts to the Cambrai area. By mid-October the decision had been made and a number of divisions allocated. Despite the continued demand for yet more troops at Ypres and a further threat to the Allied cause posed by the Italian rout at Caporetto, General Byng and his corps commanders pressed on with their plans and preparations.

Away from the rarified atmosphere of Army HQ, battalions of the 20th Division had settled in and were enjoying themselves. One chronicler of the 7/Somerset LI recalled:

'In this quiet little place time passed without incident...life
was so pleasant that the battalion wags began to wonder whether
the High Command would forget the 20th Division and leave it
*in its present sector for the duration of the war'.*1

Gradually, things did begin to change. From late October the diarist of 12/RB noted increasing activity behind the British lines and parties from other divisions arriving to stooge around. The noise of an increasing number of big guns being hauled to the front was largely disguised by bursts of well-timed fire from the divisional MGCs and a Labour Battalion was seen working close to the front lines on the Beaucamp-Villers-Plouich road. On 10 November, when COs were called to brigade conferences, a definite, distinctive buzz passed through the ranks of the division.

To add further to the speculation, in the second week of the month several battalions entrained for Plateau Station for a day's training with tanks. The 7/DCLI seem to have been the first to go, followed shortly by, among others, 12/KRRC of 60 Brigade. No one at Bray was expecting the Rifles so the battalion was forced to endure a chilly and uncomfortable night in a hastily requisitioned prisoner-of-war cage. After the 7/Somerset LI had concluded its training stint, apparently only one member remained sceptical of the tanks' potential. Although impressed by what he had seen, Captain Peard remarked: 'C'est magnifique, mais ce n'est pas La Vacquerie'.[2] With over 400 monsters amassing, tanks were of course intended to play a major and decisive role in the coming battle. They were designed to fulfil three principal functions: to fight and destroy enemy trenches, to pull aside wire obstacles strewn across tracks and roads and to act as supply and gun carriers. Two-thirds were to be employed as fighting tanks, behind which the infantry would advance and sweep through the gaps bludgeoned in the enemy wire. The cavalry too was intended to play an important role. A good deal of planning went into where the several divisions should assemble and the routes they would use to the front should a breakthrough be achieved. The Metz-Trescault and the Gouzeaucourt-Villers-Plouich roads, for example, were to be improved specifically for use by the cavalry. Beyond the British front line, those roads, together with the Gouzeaucourt-LaVacquerie road, would initially be cleared by wire-pulling tanks and then improved by cavalry reserves trained in pioneering work. Two days' supply of oats and hay were dumped at Heudicourt and concentration positions around Villers Plouich, Beaucamp and Trescault had been identified. Considerable thought was also given to ensuring supplies could be adequately maintained for all arms. RE and Pioneers would be expected to labour on the roads in the forward areas and it was anticipated that within two days the terminus of the British light railway at Gouzeaucourt could be connected with that of the German track two miles away at La Vacquerie.

Behind the lines, the village of Metz had been transformed during the summer months. By November it had become a thriving community of Nissen huts and dug outs housing battery HQ, command posts, officers' messes and administrative centres; with the coming battle, it assumed an even greater importance. From 15 November many batteries passed through its streets and silently took up positions in pits and sunken lanes to its north and east. The thick, murky weather

Flesquières Ridge

Ribécourt

6th Division

The crest of Highland Ridge between Villers-Plouich and Ribécourt (left). The 1/Leicestershire and 9/Suffolk of the 6th Division attacked down the slope to cross Plush Trench, Unseen Trench and Unseen Support and into the outskirts of Ribécourt. Beyond is the Flesquières Ridge.

helped to conceal their movement and soon huge stocks of shells, brought up by railway, were dumped alongside the guns. A 9.2-inch railway gun was shunted into a siding between the village and Gouzeaucourt Wood and, to keep the huge influx of battery horses watered, the existing facility at the sugar factory had its capacity raised form 60 to 2000 animals per hour.

General Byng insisted that on arrival none of the additional batteries should attempt to register. The artillery had made great strides since the start of the war in laying out its guns on hostile batteries by sound ranging, flash spotting and aerial observation; to achieve surprise the incoming batteries were ordered to remain silent until zero. Similarly, the concentration of tanks was achieved in secret. They were allotted lying-up positions in Gouzeaucourt, Villers-Plouich and Dessart Wood, and would move forward only shortly before zero. Their accompanying infantry were also arriving and slipping into their assault positions. In III Corps the left of the 20th Division was relieved by units of 16 Brigade, 6th Division during the night of 17-18 November and, on the following night, the left of the 12th Division took over the Gonnelieu sector from the right of the 20th.

In IV Corps sector the 51st Division had detrained at Péronne and

Territorials of the 4/Gordon Highlanders cross British trenches as they move towards the Flesquières Ridge. The 51st Division suffered badly on 20 November, largely owing to its poor cooperation with the tanks.

marched north-east to fill the line around Trescault. At night the Trescault-Metz road bulged with traffic of all descriptions; batteries hauled by tractors, tanks, vehicles, GS wagons and columns of infantry all sought their particular avenue; on the edges and in the banks and quarries, dug outs and gun pits sheltered command positions and blunt-nosed howitzers. Cavalry of 1 and 2 Brigades were scheduled to concentrate around Trescault during the late morning of 20 November and the HQ of the 51st Division was to occupy a dug out in the road junction at the south-western edge of the village during the following day. On the right of the divisional front the attack was to be led by 152 Brigade. With their right adjoining 71 Brigade on Lancaster Road, the 5/Seaforth Highlanders were to follow their tanks down the slope of the Trescault Spur to pass west of Ribécourt. Once the attack began Trescault became an area of reserve and concentration. As it was not seriously threatened during the German counter-stroke, it temporarily passes from our story.

On the left of the 6th Division's front the 1/Leicestershire and 9/Suffolk were to attack from the trenches north-east of Beaucamp towards the German outpost line (Plush Trench), pass over the Hindenburg main and support lines (Unseen Trench and Unseen Support) and on through Ribécourt. The Leicestershires' HQ was sited in Beaucamp Support, with the battalion lined up on a front of 600m

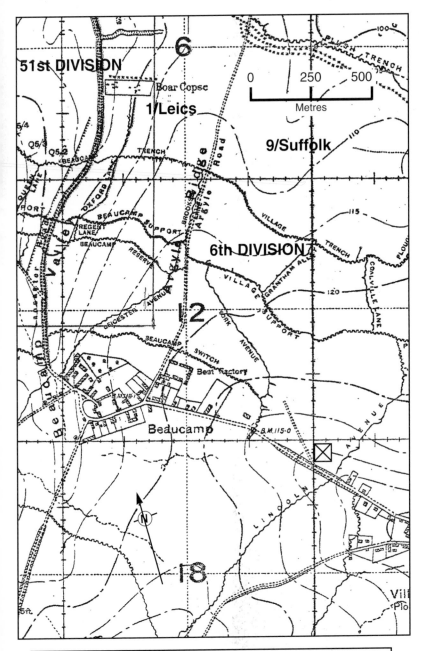

Map 13. Attack of 6th Division: 20th November 1917

Hauling sledges loaded with supplies, this tank is traversing ground somewhere near Ribécourt.

between Argyle and Lancaster Roads. Two platoons of B Company were each to advance behind a section of three tanks and take Plush Trench; other companies would pass through and go on to Unseen Support. On the right of the Leicestershire, and with its right on Barricade Road, one company of the 9/Suffolk was formed up across the entire battalion front. Once this company had taken Plush Trench and the supporting companies Unseen Trench and Support, the 9/Norfolk and two companies of the 2/Sherwood Foresters would capture Ribécourt.

To the right of the Suffolk the 8/Bedfordshire had moved up from Fifteen Ravine and was to advance on the German trenches between Barricade Road and the track along Highland Ridge which runs roughly parallel to it. The other attacking battalion of 16 Brigade, the 2/York & Lancs, filled the gap between that track and the railway running along Couillet Valley. The York & Lancs had the difficult prospect of advancing against Couillet Wood and that part of the Hindenburg system which cut through it down to the valley bottom. During the darkness of 17 November two companies had relieved 12/KRRC in Plouich Support and Rhondda Trench and prepared for the assault. The plan was for two companies to capture the Hindenburg Line between their boundary with the 8/Bedfordshire and the western edge of Couillet Wood. Another company would follow at 200 yards distance and take the main defences within the wood by a flanking attack from the west. To assist in this difficult manoeuvre, the company had one gun of the brigade's TMB attached as close support. The remaining company was delegated to clear a communication trench

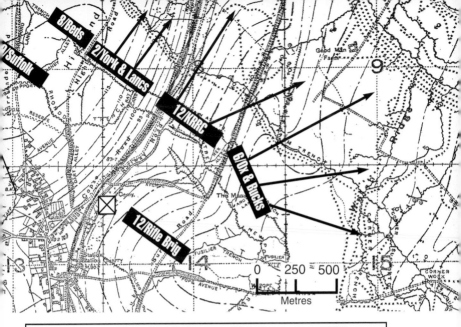

Map 14. 16 and 60 Brigades: 20th November 1917

running north-east through the wood while the 1/Buffs, with a detachment of brigade snipers, would work their way through the wood and on towards Marcoing.

With the arrival of the 6th and 12th Divisions, the 20th Division's front was reduced to extend from the Gouzeaucourt-Cambrai railway on the left to the main Péronne-Cambrai road on the right. On the left, 60 Brigade had 12/KRRC east of the railway and 6/Ox & Bucks on its right. Their objectives were Farm Trench, (the German outpost line), and Corner Trench and Support, north of La Vacquerie. Eighteen tanks of A Battalion were allotted to the two assaulting units. Behind the KRRC, 12/RB would pass through and take the main Hindenburg system. Several tanks had problems crossing the Gouzeaucourt-Villers-Plouich road and the adjacent railway; traffic became double-banked on the road and delayed 12/RB as it moved up. Nevertheless, passing batteries of 9.2-inch howitzers which had been hauled to within 1000 yards of the enemy line, the battalion pressed on through Villers-Plouich and formed up on Village Road.

On the right of 60 Brigade, 61 Brigade was to go for La Vacquerie and the trenches to its south. The 7/DCLI formed up between Welsh and Village Roads, 1500 yards due west of La Vacquerie. The first wave was to take and consolidate Corner Work and the sunken lane which it straddled to its junction with the La Vacquerie-Marcoing road. The two remaining companies of the DCLI, the 12/King's and the

99

7/KOYLI were then to advance against the Hindenburg Line. The 7/Somerset LI was told that the battalion had been specially chosen for the attack on the commanding position of La Vacquerie, the capture of which certainly held the key to the success of the right flank. The brigade was allotted 36 fighting tanks of A Battalion in addition to a section of wire-pulling tanks which would lead the way. During the chilly hours of the night preceding the attack, the tanks' officers offered shelter, drink and cigarettes to their colleagues of the Somerset.

With the tanks in position, at 6.10am the infantry moved off; ten minutes later the barrage crashed down on the unsuspecting Germans. The German response against 71 Brigade was recorded as, 'very slow and very weak...simply promiscuous shelling'.[3] The 1/Leicestershire took its objectives without difficulty and by 9.30am Battalion HQ was advanced to occupy a dug out in Unseen Trench. The battalion captured 39 prisoners of the *387th Regiment*, described later as 'not conspicuous by reason of the strength of their opposition or by their soldierly bearing'. The 9/Suffolk moved off in lines of platoon column and then, having crossed their own wire, swung out into extended order 200m from Plush Trench. Some trouble was experienced when two tanks lost direction and another two were knocked out; Lieutenant Taylor and his batman rescued another stricken tank which had become immobilised by a knife rest entangled in its track. Undeterred, D

Hyacinth ditched in a German trench west of Ribécourt on 20 November. Troops of the 1/Leicestershire stand around in idle curiosity.

Ribécourt soon after its capture on 20 November. Watched by soldiers of the Leicestershire Regiment, Scottish troops and their German captives walk westwards along the Marcoing road.

Company utilised the gaps made by the enemy in his own wire and took its objectives. By 9.05am all companies were on objectives and in touch with units to the left and right. Lieutenant-Colonel Latham, flag stick in hand, crossed No Man's Land to establish a new Battalion HQ in a former German dug out.

The next task for 71 Brigade was to take Ribécourt village. Division believed the outskirts were easily defensible although the village itself was deemed to be of little military value. The natural features however offered, in the words of a contemporary briefing 'considerable resources to a stubborn enemy'.[4] It was crossed by two ravines, 'sharp edged furrows, almost always dry',[5] and there were known to be numerous deep galleries and dug outs beneath the square. Furthermore, the church steeple was loopholed and 90 feet above the ground a concrete platform with a three foot parapet had been constructed. The village, and what might prove to be its formidable obstacles, was the objective of A Company of the 9/Norfolk. Once the village was taken, the 11/Essex, attached from 18 Brigade, would go on to the Hindenburg Support Line, known in this sector as Kaiser Trench and Kaiser Support. Colonel Prior of the Norfolk followed the second wave of tanks as they trundled across No Man's Land:

Ponderous, grunting, groaning, wobbling, these engines of war crawled and lurched their way towards the enemy lines, followed by groups of men in file...But the slowness of those tanks! It is at these moments that one itches for quickness and rapidity, and the slow, deliberate action of these monsters was exasperating.[6]

The slowness of the tanks added to the problems of the Norfolk. On its way to Ribécourt C Company had outstripped the tanks as they crossed Grand Ravine. This caused a dilemma for Prior: 'I could see parties of the enemy running through the streets...should we wait for the tanks and the three other companies?'[7] As the company was under shell fire and the enemy was showing signs of recovering from the initial shock, Prior ordered Captain Failes to take the village this side of the ravine and to hold the bridge crossing it. Failes secured his objective and soon the tanks and two other companies reached the village. With a great deal of personal satisfaction Prior watched A Company make:

...a beautiful attack on the line of houses on the left supported by a tank...attacked by sectional rushes, covering the advance by rifle fire, and I could not help feeling that my efforts at open warfare training whilst at Tinques had not been wasted...runners arrived with broad grins and puffing German cigars.[8]

There was some hand-to-hand fighting but, as the Essex passed through to assault Kaiser Trench, the Norfolk settled to consolidation.[9]

The 2/SF left Beaucamp in the wake of the Suffolk, suffering only marginally from the 'slight and wild' German barrage. Passing through the Suffolk in Unseen Trench, one company lost its tanks but pressed on with the bayonet. A runners' post was established but few messages arrived at Battalion HQ owing, as the diary recorded, 'to the rapidity of the advance'.[10] One company pushed on too far and had to be withdrawn as 14/DLI of 18 Brigade and the Guernsey LI of the 29th Division passed through. Several German pill boxes and command posts in Kaiser Trench were captured by the battalion and the Essex captured a battery of 4.2-inch guns by direct assault with rifles and Lewis guns. One enemy bunker contained a good supply of candles and the German equivalent of Tommy cookers and was assumed to have been a German Quartermaster's store. As no fuel ration came up that night, the Foresters put the cookers to good use.

A supposedly contemporary account of the Foresters' attack was written up soon after the war by Conan Doyle:

The Foresters had at least one sharp tussle before they gained their full objective. A shock battalion charged them, and there was a period of desperate fighting during which the Germans displayed valour which sometimes was almost that of fanatics. One of their companies was cut off. We offered them quarter but they would not hear of it. The last to go was a young subaltern. When he saw that all was up he drew his revolver and shot himself. As he fell I ran forward in the hope to save him, for he was a brave lad. When I got to his side he looked at me with intense hatred and tried to take aim with his pistol. It fell from his hand and he fell dead with that look of hatred still on his face.[11]

The 8/Bedfordshire too had reached all of its objectives with little difficulty. The troops went over at 6.10am 'lighting pipes and cigarettes on the way'[12] and by 7.05am Battalion received reports that the companies were in occupation of the Hindenburg Line for some 650 yards east of Barricade Road. HQ moved forward to Ridge Trench, south of Ribécourt, and reported: 'Prisoners coming in fast...all going

Troops of the Leicestershire Regiment occupying a captured trench near Ribécourt on 20 November 1917.

well, the enemy on the run'.[13] By 1.30pm a convoy of pack animals had brought up supplies of water and ammunition and the battalion, in 'high spirits and quite ready for further action',[14] busied itself in consolidation. Similarly, the 2/York & Lancs had achieved the difficult task of taking the outpost line and then swinging right into Couillet Wood. The 24 tanks allotted to the brigade had played a useful part but they were of little profit to the Buffs clearing the wood. While one company worked through the wood, the rest of the Buffs pushed on down Highland Ridge to link with the Foresters in Kaiser Support.

When considering the ground gained and the enormity of the obstacles to be overcome, casualties in the two attacking brigades of the 6th Division were negligible. An initial total of 21 killed and 91 wounded was reported by 16 Brigade and 61 killed and 242 wounded by 71 Brigade.[15]

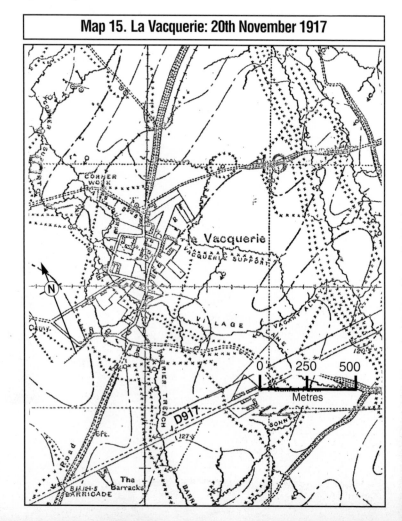

Map 15. La Vacquerie: 20th November 1917

On the eastern side of the railway, 12/KRRC advanced from Mountain Ash Trench towards Farm Trench. There was little opposition at first, although a German trench-mortar barrage around the Monument did cause trouble to the supporting companies. One company managed to capture a German canteen, replete with bountiful supplies of beer, wine and cigars. Resistance stiffened somewhat when B Company moved towards the final objective, a small mound containing a dug out just beyond the Hindenburg Support Line. The company was led by Captain·Hoare, a rigid disciplinarian with 22 years' service as rifleman and officer. On reaching the objective the company came under heavy fire from front and flank. Hoare and 14 men were killed on the mound and when the last remaining NCO, Sergeant Rowland, was wounded, Hoare's orderly, Rifleman Shepherd, took command. Shepherd, who had already that day charged a machine gun single handedly and killed its crew, dashed back over 70 yards of open bullet-swept ground to enlist the assistance of an approaching tank. Only 34 of the 97 men of the company who began the advance survived the day. Shepherd was awarded the VC.

Further up the slope and on the crest of Welsh Ridge, 6/Ox & Bucks was also making good progress. With their nine tanks the two leading companies crossed Farm Trench but then bore a little too far to the right; two platoons, helpfully but mistakenly, joined with the DCLI to take Corner Work and passed a little below La Vacquerie. The

A disabled wire-cutting tank utilised as an observation post in the Ribécourt area, 23 November 1917.

confusion was mastered and Battalion HQ moved forward to a dug out in the Hindenburg Line south of Good Man Farm. Shortly after 9am the supporting battalions began to pass through. On the left, 12/RB ran into trouble from a German machine-gun nest and TMB lodged in Good Man Farm. Captain Fraser requested the help of a nearby tank but it was knocked out about 50m from the ruined buildings. Although severely wounded, the tank's commander, Captain Richard Wain, unshipped a Lewis and charged the nest. Two platoons of the RB rushed in from the flank but Wain was hit again and died from his wounds.[16] He was awarded a posthumous VC. The battalion pushed on to secure its objectives and waited for a brigade of the 29th Division to pass through. The cellars of Good Man Farm were soon occupied by HQ of both the KRRC and the RB.

La Vacquerie and Corner Work were taken without too much difficulty by the 7/DCLI and 7/Somerset LI and, once again, a plentiful supply of German cigars was liberated from among the ruins. Captain Spark of the Somerset recalled the opening of the attack:

Five minutes before zero we moved off behind the tanks. This was the worst part of the attack, for the tanks seemed to be making an appalling noise and every moment we expected the German barrage to crash down on us. Over our front line trench we went and still no sound except the tanks' infernal noise; then carefully through the gaps in our wire; the tanks were now rattling and grunting as they increased their speed; we cursed them in whispers in our fear of being heard by Jerry! When not under fire, silence in No Man's Land had become a habit which not even a clanking tank could break! Then we were out on the damp, misty grass of No Man's Land.

Suddenly with a deafening crash our guns opened the barrage. For a moment the enemy made no sign; then enquiring lights went climbing into the sky; they seemed to be trying to discover the meaning of this extraordinary affair! Behind these lights was an inferno of bursting shrapnel, brilliant high explosive and heavy clouds of smoke.

Now it was getting pretty light, and tanks followed by small parties of infantry, could be seen on either side. Soon German shells began to scream and moan overhead, and looking back we saw them bursting on our front line. Then I heard the rattle of a machine gun and the sinister noise of bullets ripping past. From this point everything seemed unreal to me. I felt no fear but only a vague curiosity. It all seemed so impersonal and as if I were merely a spectator. I had no conscious thought, but little scenes impressed themselves on my mind. I noticed neither time, space nor noise, but only incidents.[17]

South of the Cambrai road, 36 Brigade had advanced against Barrier Trench and Sonnet Farm. The 7/Sussex led the way with the 9/RF supporting its left. To conform with the Somersets' attack on La Vacquerie, two companies of the 8/RF took the trenches north of Sonnet Farm. The other two brigades of the 12th Division moved across the main Hindenburg Line and on to the Bonavis Ridge.

The 12/King's passed through the Somerset to continue the advance; shortly afterwards, the Canadian Cavalry Brigade, horse artillery and limbers began to trot through La Vacquerie and down the sunken lane beyond. During the morning the 1/Essex of 88 Brigade, accompanied by four tanks, passed down La Vacquerie Valley having earlier run into trouble against a German battery on Welsh Ridge. The reserve brigade of the 20th Division had moved up to the ridge and La Vacquerie to support the gains made by 60 and 61 Brigades; it was in turn leapfrogged by the Essex and the 4/Worcestershire on their way to Masnières. To the north, 87 Brigade in the centre of the 29th Division, made its way towards Marcoing by way of Couillet Valley, while 86 Brigade moved through 16 Brigade west of the railway. Also on the move along Couillet Valley were the Secunderabad and Ambala Brigades of the 5th Cavalry Division, the road, as planned, having been prepared by the cavalry's Pioneers.

It had been a remarkably successful day for Third Army, but the

Troops, possibly of a Pioneer battalion, and mules follow the advance towards La Vacquerie on the opening day of the Battle of Cambrai.

Awaiting the call to advance through the Hindenburg Line, Lancers assemble on the Metz-Trescault road. Limbers pass on the left to deliver their cargoes in Ribécourt.

coming of darkness, the blocked roads and stiffening German resistance combined to prevent the really decisive breakthrough; Byng's hope that the situation would have been sufficiently satisfactory to throw in the cavalry had proved false. Too much had to be done to improve communications before the breaches in the German defences could be fully exploited. Acknowledging the amount of work needed on forward roads and tracks, the prevailing weather and the enormous quantities of supplies to be carried up, the official historian recorded: 'Despite their utmost exertions the field companies and other RE units, pioneer battalions and labour contingents were taxed far beyond their powers'.[18] Consequently, when it was accepted that nothing more could be achieved that day, orders were issued for the cavalry to bivouac in allotted areas; Welsh Ridge, between Good Man Farm and Corner Work, became the chilly, damp overnight home for 3, 5 and Lucknow Cavalry Brigades.

For the subsequent nine days Beaucamp, Villers-Plouich and the ridges remained behind the British lines. They became choked with gun batteries, dressing stations, transport lines and troops moving to and from the front. Amid the constant flow of traffic, men and horse, Engineers, Pioneers and Labour battalions struggled to keep the roads passable; the weather might have been worse, but it was, after all, late November. The Germans recovered well and contained the British advance among the shattered trees of Bourlon Wood. The battle had, as so many earlier attempts, reverted to a slogging match of attrition. Then, in the murk of an early morning, the Germans launched their counter-stroke.

Most of the battalions which had opened the offensive on 20 November had spent the intervening period alternately resting, working on defences, or fighting. The anticipated breakthroughs at Masnières and Marcoing had not materialised and there was increasing concern among some senior commanders that a counter-attack was inevitable. Lieutenant-General Snow even anticipated where the blow would fall. Banteux Ravine marked the boundary between the 55th Division of VII Corps and the 12th Division of III Corps. As the 55th had not advanced on 20 November, the 12th Division held the southern shoulder of a pronounced salient along the Bonavis Ridge. The 12th did not command observation over the canal crossings and its lines of communication ran virtually parallel to its front. If the enemy did advance up Banteux Ravine he could attack the right flank of the 12th or surge on towards Gouzeaucourt at the end of the ravine. If that village, well to the rear of the British front positions, was taken, the

Fort Garry Horse returning from their charge at Masnières on 20 November. A breakdown of communication and poor intelligence meant that B Squadron became isolated from the rest of the regiment. It surged through the German wire, attacked a battery and captured several prisoners. It eventually stampeded its horses and made its way back on foot. Lieutenant H. Strachan was awarded the VC for his gallantry and leadership.

routes to Péronne and Metz would be open.

When it came, the German attack was overwhelming. The sorely stretched and under strength 5/South Lancashire, left battalion of the 55th Division, was swept away in the enemy drive on Gouzeaucourt. The right of the 12th Division fared little better and by 9am the Germans were in Gouzeaucourt. Little work had been done to prepare the village for defence but it did contain five batteries of heavy howitzers, one company of Pioneers of the 11/DLI and the transport of one brigade of the 6th Division. In addition, details of several other units were forced back into the village as the Germans poured over the Quentin Ridge. To the south-west, Vincent's Force, comprising a mixture of cyclists, infantry, cavalry, Pioneers and RE, held Révelon Ridge; with the object of supporting Vincent's left flank, an old trench about 1000 yards west of Gouzeaucourt was manned with an assortment of troops. Captain Tollit, adjutant of the Pioneers, discovered an abandoned staff car on the Fins road; borrowing guns and ammunition from several tanks he utilised the car to carry them forward to his motley command of men from at least five different regiments.

The Quartermasters of 18 Brigade in Gouzeaucourt had their wagons packed and away before the Germans had fully occupied the village. Leaving the Quartermaster and 44 men of the section in Gouzeaucourt, Lieutenant Fetherstonhaugh of the 11/Essex led the first line transport off to Fins. Under the command of Captain and QM Roberts, these men scrambled into an old trench alongside the Gouzeaucourt-Fins road. On receipt of information that the enemy was advancing from the east rather than the south-east, Roberts took his men to join with a similar number of transport details of the 1/West Yorkshire and 2/DLI. The drivers were soon in action and provided flank protection to the 1/Irish Guards when they made their attack towards Gonnelieu. In the early hours of 1 December, the three units and their respective Quartermasters were finally relieved and went off in search of their battalions.

The Germans began to shell the forward positions of the 12th Division at about 6.45am on 30 November; the situation soon became so confused that within five hours battalions of 35 Brigade fell back on Bleak Trench and Bleak Support. A little later, when it was realised that the Germans were already in possession of Gonnelieu and Gouzeaucourt to their right rear, the 9/Essex and 7/Suffolk withdrew further; they took up a position south of La Vacquerie on Cemetery Ridge. What was left of the 7/Norfolk withdrew towards the Cambrai

Battle traffic and cavalry
manoeuvre along the
Trescault road near
Ribécourt, 22 November
1917.   IWM Q6311

road where it was incorporated within the 9/RF. The two Fusilier battalions of 36 Brigade were currently manning trenches immediately south of the Cambrai road. Under the command of Lieutenant-Colonel Someren, the 9/RF held the southern end of Pelican Trench while its sister battalion, the 8th, held the northern end and Sonnet Farm. As they were the focus of repeated enemy attacks towards La Vacquerie on 30 November, the two battalions suffered badly. Several times the Fusiliers counter-attacked but when the Germans broke through to the right rear of the 8th Battalion, its two front companies were cut off. D Company, ordered up to assist the forward two, was also overwhelmed and withdrew on Battalion HQ. When the Germans were only 50 yards from HQ, Lieutenant-Colonel Elliott-Cooper collected about 120 men and led them in a bayonet charge. Cheering as they went, the Fusiliers chased the enemy for over 600 yards back across the Bonavis Ridge, releasing in the advance members of D Company who had earlier been captured. However, on seeing the huge numbers of German troops advancing beyond the ridge, Elliott-Cooper ordered a withdrawal. He was hit, captured and died as a prisoner of war.[19] That day the battalion lost ten officers and 247 men, a figure almost matched by the 9th Battalion. This unit lost an entire company when three strong points covering Bleak House were surrounded and overwhelmed. On 1 December the Germans made seven attempts to cross the Cambrai road and get on towards La Vacquerie; on each occasion they were repulsed by the dwindling number of Fusiliers and Norfolk. Eventually their bomb supply was exhausted and the remnant was forced to withdraw to a point just north of the main road. The Fusiliers' chronicler believed that, although they received no rations or supplies, they were the only troops south of the Cambrai road to retain their positions for two days.[20]

North of the main road, another German thrust towards La Vacquerie, this time against the front of the 20th Division, came about one hour after the attack along Banteux Ravine. The Division's reserve brigade had been in Villers-Plouich and was ordered up to hold a line on the Quentin Ridge. Confusion and counter-order resulted in a disjointed attack by 60 Brigade, firstly by the 6/KSLI, which took Farnham Quarry, and then by the 6/Ox & Bucks which attacked southwards on the left of the Shropshire across the Cambrai road towards Gonnelieu. The Ox & Bucks connected with the right of 12/RB which had advanced as far as a communication trench running between the main road and the north-west side of Gonnelieu; 12/KRRC had simultaneously moved forward on the extreme left to

**German field guns captured by the 11/Essex on 20 November. This photo
was taken two days later, purportedly at Ribécourt.** IWM Q6313

cover the southern approaches to La Vacquerie. Facing mainly south
and south-east, 60 Brigade was unsure of developments to its front and
rear. It was in touch with 1 Guards Brigade on the right and with units
of 35 Brigade, 12th Division, on the left. But what had befallen 37
Brigade around Bonavis and Pam Pam Farms was, at the time, largely
speculative.

The truth was that the 7/East Surrey and 6/West Kent had been
virtually wiped out. What remnants survived the German
bombardment and infantry onslaught rallied with three companies of
the 6/Buffs north-west of Pam Pam Farm. Here, with the assistance of
the 37th MGC and 179 Army Brigade RFA, they poured a devastating
fire into the Germans advancing down the slope of the Bonavis Ridge
towards La Vacquerie. However, weight of numbers, lack of
ammunition and the danger of envelopment told and the few hundred
survivors of 37 Brigade fell back towards La Vacquerie; here they
gained touch with other elements of the 12th Division which had
joined with 12/KRRC of 60 Brigade.

Troops of the 20th Division were having an equally torrid time.
Covering the front from Lateau Wood to a little south of Masnières, 59
Brigade on the right and 61 Brigade on the left had borne the brunt of
a massive German thrust. The 10th and 11/KRRC were caught in a
salient attacked across its base. On the right, the 10th was
overwhelmed, ending the day with a strength of four officers and 16
men; on its left, the forward company of the 11th was never seen again.
Those that were left of the other companies attempted to make a

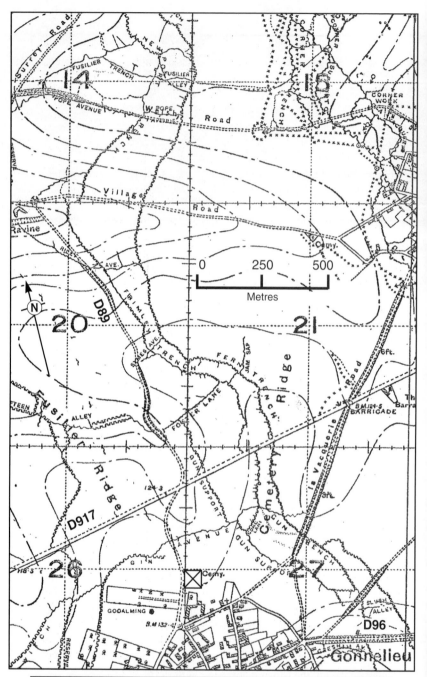

Map 16. Fusilier and Cemetery Ridges: 20th November 1917

fighting withdrawal towards La Vacquerie. A little to the rear, 10/RB was surprised and virtually annihilated; all officers at Battalion HQ became casualties or prisoners. The survivors, who amounted to Captain Pegler, four officers and 20 men, joined with a party of the 7/DCLI 1000 yards east of La Vacquerie. The party was attached to 11/RB, then holding a reserve position in front of the Hindenburg Support system. Attacked four times during the course of the morning, the battalion dispersed the Germans by rifle and Lewis gun fire but, unsure of its flanks and with rumours that La Vacquerie to its rear had fallen, the RB hung on precariously to what had become the 20th Division's foremost positions.

The more immediate threat to La Vacquerie however lay not from the east, but from the south. Battalions of 60 Brigade, remaining in touch with the Guards on the right, still held positions largely north of the Cambrai road. Having moved from Fifteen Ravine early on 30 November, 12/RB worked its way up the shallow valley and onto Fusilier Ridge. By 10.30am it deployed in Gin Avenue, a long communication trench south-east of the Cambrai road. On arrival it discovered a few Pioneers of the 5/Northants in a forward position on its right, while parties of 12/KRRC were seen about 400 yards to the left. By dusk, 6/Ox & Bucks had advanced astride the Gouzeaucourt-Gonnelieu road and was in touch with 12/RB. On the left, 12/KRRC held a very extended front stretching from where the old British line crossed the Cambrai road on the crest of Cemetery Ridge, to the east of La Vacquerie. At about 10.30am approximately 150 men of 35 Brigade who, according to the war diary were 'retiring in the worst disorder'[21], were halted and told to dig in a few metres south of La Vacquerie cemetery: 'Steps were taken to ensure that any further movement on their part, except to advance, a very unlikely contingency, should be met with immediate punishment'.[22] The KRRC deployed three companies in the village and another on the crest to command the approaches up the shallow valley from the south-east. One company could muster only 39 rifles; the others were only marginally stronger. Battalion HQ, which was established in Foster Lane, an old British communication trench running north of the Cambrai road between Fusilier and Cemetery Ridges, enjoyed the somewhat dubious protection of one company of the 9/Essex. According to the Rifles the morale of the Essex was 'poor',[23] an assessment which was proved correct next morning when a direct frontal attack on Foster Lane compelled Battalion HQ to withdraw to the other side of the Gonnelieu-Villers-Plouich road. To the bewilderment and annoyance of the Rifles, half of the Essex, who had all been ordered to stay where they were, doubled across the road at their heels.

During the evening of 30 November a patrol of 12/RB crossed the Cambrai road and cautiously attempted to penetrate Gonnelieu. It soon ran into difficulty and had to fight its way back, attracting on the way some stranded RE of the 12th Division. The engineers were immediately put to work laying wire in advance of the RB's trenches. The real threat came at about 8.30am on 1 December when the Guards were driven from their tenuous hold of a section of Gonnelieu. Germans poured towards the beleaguered RB and KRRC who were both by now very weak in numbers. With only one unwounded officer in the three forward companies, the CSM of B Company 12/RB, organised a counter-attack on his own initiative. He was last seen with a handful of men advancing towards Gonnelieu cemetery against vastly superior numbers. Repeated German attacks against Fusilier Ridge were repulsed by Captain Williams and his men who maintained a ferocious fire against the enemy attempting to force their way through the engineers' wire. Having fired off most of its ammunition, Williams' company threw out a defensive flank on the left. Next, Battalion HQ and C Company joined in the action. At a range of 600m, they used Vickers, Lewis guns and rifles to fire hundreds of rounds into hordes of advancing Germans. Captain Lloyd's company of the KRRC fired into the right flank of the wedge that the Germans were trying to drive between the two battalions. Another strong thrust moving above ground and up Barrier Trench threatened La Vacquerie. The German bombers made progress, forcing the Rifles back 70m, before a counter-attack and close-quarter fighting temporarily restored

British soldiers converse in the recently captured village of Marcoing. Troops of the 29th Division reached the village on the first day of the battle. It was evacuated on the night of 3-4 December.

Taken on 29 November 1917, this photo shows British troops watching as a tank hauls in a captured 5.9" naval gun. Although the official caption claims it to be at Ribécourt, it is more likely to be Havrincourt Wood.

the situation: 'Their bombers appeared to be well trained, but our men had been told to hold that village at all costs; and, profiting by the example set by their officers and NCOs, they carried out their orders'.[24]

Pressure upon the RB, KRRC and Ox & Bucks further west remained severe all day. Numerous German snipers and a small field gun firing over open sights persistently harassed and annoyed the defenders of La Vacquerie. When a local attack drove in its forward company, the Ox & Bucks were forced to give ground, recrossing the main road to establish a new line from Farnham Quarry east to the end of Flag Ravine. An attack by 1/Grenadier Guards from Fifteen and Flag Ravines towards Gonnelieu cemetery and Foster Lane, together with a party of the RB who attached themselves to the Grenadiers, pushed the Germans back across the Cambrai road and earned a little respite. At dusk on 1 December the positions of 60 Brigade had been maintained but:

The situation did not present a happy picture. The men who had started on 30 November far from fresh after nine strenuous days, were now much exhausted. The battalion was holding a wide front - far greater than that properly allotted to it, including one important village and on the flank of another – no less important. Not a single man remained in reserve or even in local support.[25]

117

However, relief for the sorely tried battalions of 60 Brigade was on its way. As the Guards took over the front held by the Ox & Bucks and 12/RB, two battalions of 183 Brigade moved up to relieve 12/KRRC. The 61st Division later extended its line north-east of La Vacquerie to take over the positions of 61 Brigade and whatever troops of the 12th Division could be located. Not that there was much of 61 Brigade to relieve. On 30 November the 7/Somerset LI had been all but wiped out on the eastern slope of Welsh Ridge, its 60 survivors falling back to the Hindenburg Line then being held by the 7/KOYLI. The 12/King's had fared even worse than the Somerset, and the DCLI only marginally better. The commanding officers of these two battalions were killed on 1 December and that of the Somerset wounded. Consequently, a composite battalion comprising 30 of the King's, 60 Somerset, 140 Cornwall, 60 RE of the 84th Field Company and 320 KOYLI fell under the command of the OC KOYLI.

To the north-east, troops of the 29th Division were preparing to withdraw from an awkward salient east of Marcoing. The division had not been heavily involved in the first two days of the German counter-offensive, although 88 Brigade did attack across the lower slopes of Welsh Ridge to drive the Germans back across the eastern end of La Vacquerie Valley. The valley itself was full of artillery; should the enemy use it as cover for another attack on the village, the many batteries would be in immediate danger of capture. During 2 December the 29th Division was holding new positions, largely in and around the Hindenburg Support Line; on its left the 6th Division was maintaining its hold around Cantaing and Folie Wood. The next serious drive by the enemy against III Corps was once more against La Vacquerie.

The second line South Midland Territorials of the 61st Division arrived at Bapaume by train at 11am on 30 November. A fleet of lorries carried them to Ruyaulcourt, where they debussed and marched to Havrincourt Wood. While waiting to move up to the ridge, the 2/5th Gloucestershire had a nasty taste of what lay in store. Sixteen men of D Company were killed and 53 wounded when a German plane scored a direct hit on an ammunition dump near to its assembly area. When 183 Brigade relieved the exhausted 20th Division its brigadier had originally intended to hold the front line at La Vacquerie with three battalions but, when he saw the unsatisfactory position especially to the south and south-west of the village, two companies of the fourth battalion were also called up and put into the line. East of the village a nasty salient existed where the trenches of the Hindenburg front system crossed the British defensive line. The 2/4th and 2/6th

Gloucestershire held the apex of the salient, with the 2/7th and 2/8th Worcestershire on either flank. At dawn on 2 December the Germans attacked the angle of the salient but were largely repulsed. A furious bombardment of the village preceded another major assault which drove the Gloucestershire battalions back almost to the eastern outskirts of La Vacquerie. During the night, 182 Brigade relieved the remnants of 61 Brigade holding the further slopes of Welsh Ridge. Soon after dawn on 3 December the 2/5th Warwickshire, which had been lent to 183 Brigade, tried and failed to regain the trenches lost the previous afternoon. This attempt was followed almost immediately by another strong German assault which swept over the the two Gloucestershire battalions and into La Vacquerie. This attack, which had worked up Barrier Trench, Village Lane and over the open, sealed the fate of the village. The redoubt at Corner Work, however, resisted. Comprised of a mixture of survivors of the two Gloucestershire battalions, some 2/8th Worcestershire and elements of the 2/5th Warwickshire, the garrison fought on all day. However, as evening approached and German bombers progressed up communication trenches either side of the redoubt, the officers began to destroy maps and papers.

Unbeknown to the weary garrison, help was at hand. Having

Gunners and infantry show off a donkey captured from the Germans near Ribécourt on 20 November.

reconnoitred the best route towards the redoubt, a patrol of the 2/8 Worcestershire returned to its own lines to bring up the remainder of its company. The Worcesters cleared the enemy from Corner Support and fought their way into Corner Work. Insufficient troops remained to attempt the recapture of La Vacquerie itself so, with the arrival at night of the 2/4th Berkshire to consolidate, the 61st Division accepted the existing situation.

To the north-east of the village and on the southern slope of Welsh Ridge, 182 Brigade was fighting to maintain its grip on the sunken lane which ran north-west across the ridge to the Villers-Plouich-Marcoing road in Couillet Valley. Repeated German attacks along a communication trench called Ostrich Avenue were repulsed by the 2/7 Warwickshire but once La Vacquerie had fallen, the Warwicks came under fire from their right rear. On 4 December renewed attacks on Ostrich Avenue continued to increase the pressure on the three Warwickshire battalions but they held their positions and hoped for relief. On 5 December the enemy again advanced in hordes and although the Warwickshires retained their tenuous grip on Ostrich Avenue, further sections of the Hindenburg Line fell into German hands. At night however, 109 Brigade of the 36th Division relieved two tired battalions of 182 Brigade. The survivors of the 2/7th Warwickshire supported an attack by the 9/Inniskilling Fusiliers on 6 December, an action for which Second Lieutenant Emerson was awarded a posthumous VC; but it was an assault by the 11/Inniskilling the following day which finally forced the Germans from the maze of trenches on the higher slopes of Welsh Ridge.

By that time, although fighting elsewhere on the Cambrai front had died down, the decision had been made to withdraw British forces to the Flesquières Ridge. After dusk on 4 December gun teams streamed up through Trescault, Ribécourt, Gouzeaucourt, Villers-Plouich and Beaucamp to haul away the forward batteries. Burdened by equipment and salvage, battalions of the 6th and 29th Divisions withdrew to rest as those of the 36th Division manned the former Hindenburg Support system between Ribécourt and Marcoing. From there the line ran across the eastern slopes of Highland Ridge before next turning south-west to pass along the crest of Welsh Ridge and then back towards Gouzeaucourt. By 7 December the British occupied what they had determined should be their winter lines and activity did markedly decrease. On one quiet night in the middle of the month Second Lieutenant Lake of the 2/5th Gloucestershire even managed to slip between the German defences in and around La Vacquerie to spend

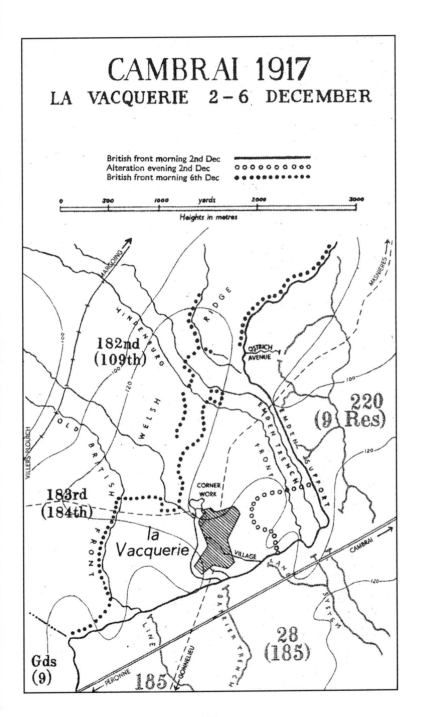

CAMBRAI 1917
LA VACQUERIE 2-6 DECEMBER

British front morning 2nd Dec ——————
Alteration evening 2nd Dec ∘∘∘∘∘∘∘∘∘
British front morning 6th Dec ••••••••••••

0   500   1000   yards   2000   3000

Heights in metres

182nd
(109th)

OSTRICH
AVENUE

220
(9 Res)

183rd
(184th)

CORNER
WORK

la
Vacquerie

VILLAGE

CAMBRAI

HINDENBURG

RIDGE

WELSH

EMDEN TRENCH

FRONT

SUPPORT

OLD BRITISH FRONT

VILLERS-PLOUICH

MARCOING

MASNIÈRES

28
(185)

Gds
(9)

PERONNE

185

GONNELIEU

BARRIER TRENCH

LINE

SYSTEM

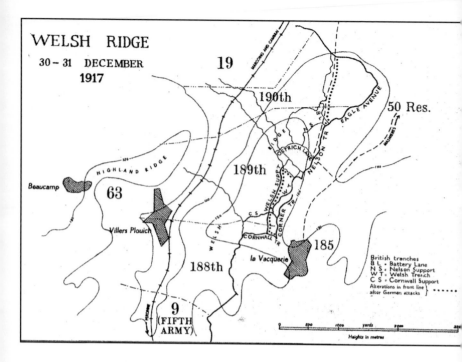

WELSH RIDGE

30 – 31 DECEMBER
1917

19

190th

50 Res.

189th

HIGHLAND RIDGE

Beaucamp

63

Villers Plouich

la Vacquerie

185

188th

British trenches
B L = Battery Lane
N S = Nelson Support
W T = Welsh Trench
C S = Cornwall Support
Alterations in front line
after German attacks

9
(FIFTH
ARMY)

Heights in metres

some considerable time, unmolested by German sentries, exploring the village. However, slack as this may have been on the part of the Germans, they were not yet quite ready to pull down the winter shutters on Welsh Ridge.

Two days before Christmas, the 63rd (Royal Naval) Division completed its relief of the 36th and 61st Divisions and occupied the whole of Welsh Ridge. In order to cover the divisional front of nearly 7000 yards the division was compelled to employ all three brigades, each with two battalions up, in the forward positions. They manned an area consisting of a welter of shattered trenches, most of which, owing to the vicissitudes of the previous weeks, were not ideally sited for defence. The weather was cold and snowy, making improvements to the wire and trenches difficult. The 25 field batteries covering the divisional front were in pits east of Gouzeaucourt Wood; during the night of 29-30 December these positions were drenched in relentless showers of gas. At 6.30am an intense barrage of howitzer shells and trench-mortar bombs erupted upon the British front positions. Lieutenant-Commander Shaw-Stewart of the Hood Battalion was killed and a little later Commander West and Lieutenant-Commander Campbell of the Howe Battalion were also mortally hit. Clad in white smocks and carrying flammenwerfers, German infantry attacked the junctions of Hood and the 7/RF and Drake and Howe. In the latter's sector, Corner Trench and Welsh Trench were lost, thus giving the enemy observation down the western slope to Villers-Plouich. The Howe Battalion responded by attempting to bomb along Cornwall Trench and Cornwall Support but failed to dislodge the enemy. So too did a counter-attack by two companies drawn from Drake and Nelson against Welsh Support. The trench was later regained during the afternoon in an action which recovered the crest for the loss of only three men and prompted a congratulatory telegram from Sir Douglas Haig.

After one company had been all but wiped out, the right battalion of 190 Brigade, the 7/RF, was forced out of Eagle Trench. There were no communication trenches down which the survivors could withdraw and attempts to retire over ground were frustrated by extant belts of old German wire. On the left of the Fusiliers the 4/KSLI was attacked by a party approaching along a sunken lane running up from Masnières, and was pushed back from its forward positions in the Hindenburg Support Line. Two companies cooperated with a partially successful counter-attack by the Artists Rifles, but the situation was more properly retrieved when Lieutenant Morley and ten men expelled the Germans from a trench by using a ready supply of enemy stick bombs. Morley, who was killed by a stray when returning to Battalion HQ, was recommended for a VC. Although the battalion was awarded 17 DCMs and MMs for the day's work, Morley received only a mention in despatches. Both battalions had suffered badly. The Fusiliers lost nine officers and 244 other ranks so, with a trench strength of only 11 officers and 167 other ranks, the battalion was temporarily amalgamated with the Artists. Meanwhile, in the centre of the divisional front, Hood had counter-attacked against Ostrich Trench. An initial success turned later to disappointment and withdrawal when the sailors were assaulted from both flanks.

At night the battle died down. Shelling continued and early next morning the enemy attempted an assault against a company of Hawke. Thirty men of Hood's D Company were killed or captured when they went to the assistance of Howe, but the worst was now over. Although desultory shelling was maintained by both sides, there was time for the Naval Division to take stock and repair its broken trenches. Fifteen German battalions had attempted to throw the division from Welsh Ridge, but at a cost of 1400 casualties, its soldiers and sailors had held on to its shell-pocked slopes.

NOTES

1. E.Wyrall, *The Somerset Light Infantry, 1914-1919*, p.227
2. Scrap book of the 7/Somerset L.I. (no author). p.94
3. H.Wylly, *The 1st and 2nd Leicestershire Regiment in the Great War*, p.54
4. J.Burrows, *Essex Units in the War*, p.341
5. Ibid
6. L.Petre, *History of the Norfolk Regiment*, Vol.II. p.274-5
7. Ibid
8. Ibid
9.   Lance Corporal McBeath, 1/5th Seaforth Highlanders, won the VC for his bravery in silencing German machine guns and capturing the HQ of a German battalion in Ribécourt. Enemy snipers in the village did hold out for some hours after Ribécourt had fallen. They caused some discomfort to the cavalry. The Marquess of Anglesey, *A History of the British Cavalry 1816-1919*, Volume 8 covers in absorbing detail the role and activities of the cavalry during the battle.
10. War diary 2/Sherwood Foresters. WO.95.1624
11. H.Wylly, *The 1st & 2nd Battalions of the Sherwood Foresters,* p.153
12. War diary 8/Bedfordshire. WO.95.1611
13. Ibid
14. Ibid
15. Battalion losses in 71 Brigade were later reported as:
1/Leicestershire, 6 dead, 46 wounded
2/SF, 9 dead, 31 wounded
9/Suffolk, 8 dead, 59 wounded
9/Norfolk, 32 dead, 61 wounded
16. Captain Richard Wain's body was not later identified. He is commemorated on the Cambrai memorial.
17. Scrap book of 7/Somerset L.I. op.cit. p.95-96
18. Official History, *Battle of Cambrai*, p.90
19. Lieutenant-Colonel Neville Elliot-Cooper, VC, DSO, MC, died at Hanover on 11 February 1918 of wounds received on 30 November. He is buried in Hamburg.
20. Scott & Brumwell, *The History of the 12th Division,* p.159, give the casualty figures for 30 November as 164 officers and 3362 other ranks – ie over 50% of the division's actual strength.
21. War diary 12/KRRC. op.cit.
22. Ibid
23. Ibid
24. Ibid
25. Ibid

Chapter Six

THE GERMAN OFFENSIVE

After the tumult of November and December, the Villers-Plouich sector in January 1918 reverted to its former fairly quiet self. The weather did not encourage offensive action but it did take a steady toll of men. During a two week period early in the month, the 4/KSLI on Welsh Ridge had 180 cases of trench feet and posts were of necessity normally relieved every 24 hours. Work, frequently hampered by thawing snow and freezing ice, continued on improving the defences. During February the weather improved somewhat and the divisions holding the sector, the 2nd, 19th and Royal Naval, underwent a reorganisation of the Corps' front. Like most other British divisions on the Western Front, they also experienced the loss of three battalions. The reduction of brigades from four to three battalions was blamed on contemporary manpower shortages. One result of such shortages was to make units such as the 1/Berkshire spend 13 successive days on the unfriendly, lacerated slopes, of Welsh Ridge.

German troops haul a heavy howitzer into position in preparation for their March offensive. A bombardment by over 6000 guns preceded the infantry assault.

There was a widespread anticipation within the BEF that the enemy was about to launch a major offensive. What was uncertain was exactly when and where the blow would fall. A test barrage was fired on the battery and front positions of the Naval Division on 8 March, but the greatest damage was done by gas barrages on a succession of nights. Thousands of phosgene and mustard gas shells drenched Farm and Fifteen Ravines, the low ground of Villers-Plouich and the ruins of Beaucamp. On Highland Ridge the 7/RF lost 250 men in two nights and the Naval Division as a whole had over 2000 gas casualties between 12-20 March. The 2nd Division lost 400 men on 12 March and over 700 the following night. The commanding officer of 1/KRRC witnessed scores of blinded and vomiting men when he toured the battalion positions on 13 March. That night his battalion suffered the loss of seven officers and 270 other ranks. Knowing that men would take between four to six weeks to recover, it seemed as if the enemy was 'deliberately thinning out his potential enemies'.[1] If this was his objective, he were meeting with significant success; the trench strength of 99 Brigade on 15 March was reckoned to amount to about 600 all ranks.

Patrols were regularly despatched to try to obtain identification of the enemy in the trenches opposite. On 18 March, under a barrage of artillery and trench-mortar shells, Second Lieutenant Fish and 11 men of the 17/RF entered the German trenches near La Vacquerie. Fish grabbed a German but the prisoner was promptly shot by one of the

German troops, complete with home comforts, relaxing in the Hindenburg Line.

Fusiliers. At least ten of the enemy were killed and the raiders returned with only several pairs of epaulettes cut from their uniforms. As the battalion war diary laconically recorded: 'No live Germans were taken owing to the keenness of our men'.[2] On 20 March the Fusiliers observed a number of German staff officers in front line positions and 'hundreds of men were seen entering and leaving the trenches in full pack'.[3] On the assumption that the German offensive was imminent, front line posts on Fusilier Ridge were withdrawn by the 9th Division. Fifteen Ravine marked the boundary between the 9th Division, VII Corps, Fifth Army and the 47th Division, V Corps, Third Army. A subsequent alleged lack of cooperation between the two divisions caused immediate difficulties when the Germans struck and an acrimonious row after the war. On 21 March two brigades of the London Division held the front positions on Welsh Ridge; the reserve line, manned by the third brigade, was on Highland Ridge. On its left and on a three brigade front, the Naval Division occupied the Hindenburg Support Line in front of Ribécourt and the British trenches as far as Flesquières.

On 21 March the enemy did not launch any serious attack against V Corps' front. He maintained instead an almost constant barrage of gas and HE, punctuated at intervals by strong fighting patrols which encroached close to the British trenches. Although communications were cut, the 47th and Naval Divisions did not suffer unduly and local counter-attacks usually restored any threatened position. For example, the 1/17th London held the area around the Monument and Surrey Road. A trench mortar bombardment practically obliterated the forward posts near Good Man Farm and, under cover of smoke, the enemy rushed several Lewis gun posts in Welsh Support and Farm Trench. Farm Trench was recovered during the afternoon but another counter-attack in conjunction with the London Irish was cancelled and replaced by an order warning the battalion to be prepared to move back to the Villers-Plouich-Ribécourt road on Highland Ridge. Worrying information had arrived at Division that, to their north and south, units of Third and Fifth Armies were in retreat. The Naval and London Brigades were ordered to withdraw, first to their support lines and then later to reserve positions near Dessart Wood and Metz. Before retiring, the London Irish on Highland Ridge repulsed three determined attacks by Germans emerging from Couillet Wood and Villers-Plouich. When a fourth developed, the Irish counter-attacked, cutting off the Germans and annihilating them save for seven who were brought in as prisoners.

The following days were those of confusion and frustration. The two divisions resented the fact that, although they had not lost any ground, they had been compelled to withdraw. To make matters worse, the reserve lines around Metz were far from complete. When the 7/RF moved back through Trescault and into position in Metz Switch they discovered:

> *A group of trenches two feet deep, no field of fire and no dug outs – no cover and no communications. There was no water, no transport and little ammunition; and when the Germans were seen advancing in the morning, the battalion was ordered to retire once more.*4

The 9th Division's evacuation of Gouzeaucourt during the night of 21-22 March exposed the right flank of V Corps. The village, which since its recapture by the Guards had again become a bulging collection of batteries, dressing stations, dumps and transport lines, was abandoned once Gauche Wood, Chapel Hill and Vaucellette Farm to the south-east had been swept away. Further north, Beaucamp, Ribécourt and Trescault were evacuated by the night of 22-23 March. The ruined villages and their adjoining disembowelled fields, which for 11 months had been in the possession of Fourth, Third and Fifth Armies, once again reverted to German occupation.

NOTES
1. E.Wyrall, *The History of the Second Division*, Vol.II. p.529
2. War diary 17/Royal Fusiliers
3. H.O'Neill, *The Royal Fusiliers in the Great War*, p.239
4. Ibid. p.238

Troops of an East Lancashire battalion marching through Metz in January 1918.
IWM Q8384

Chapter Seven

RECAPTURING THE RIDGES

In the late summer of 1918 Allied forces again approached Villers-Plouich and its accompanying ridges. Metz fell to the 1st Otago Regiment of the New Zealand Division on 6 September and the ridge overlooking Gouzeaucourt Wood from the west shortly after. However, the next stage of the advance towards the Hindenburg Line was to prove exceedingly difficult and costly. The Germans made determined efforts to keep the British forces from the high ground east of Trescault, Beaucamp and Gouzeaucourt and it was not until the end of the month that the enemy was finally expelled from La Vacquerie and Ribécourt.

The Germans utilised the former British reserve positions to the west of the villages and ridges. When approaching them, British forces had first to take what had been their own third line support trenches, then the main defences of their old third line; beyond those lay the former British second and front systems. The number of old gun pits, assembly trenches, main fire trenches and wire provided the Germans with formidable defensive positions. Many of them when originally sited had been dug on reverse slopes but, with the danger now approaching from the opposite direction, they no longer enjoyed that advantage. Nevertheless, climbing the rises to Trescault and Beaucamp

The scene of dreadful carnage in September 1918, the fields between Beaucamp and Gouzeaucourt have returned to more peaceful purposes. The eastern edge of Gouzeaucourt Wood is right, the trees marking Dead Man's Corner, centre left, and the small clump of bushes growing on Caesar's Camp beyond.

and getting over the crests to drop into Villers-Plouich and Gouzeaucourt was to involve a series of bloody, set-piece engagements.

Lying between the Révelon-Gouzeaucourt and Fins-Gouzeaucourt roads, Heather Support and Heather Trench covered the south-western approaches to Gouzeaucourt. North of the Fins-Gouzeaucourt road these two trenches were known as African Support and African Trench. They ran roughly north-south, crossing the Metz-Gouzeaucourt road approximately mid-way between Gouzeaucourt village and its wood. African Trench cut along the eastern brow of the ridge, with African Support on the western slope commanding the wood. Further north beyond Dead Man's Corner, Lincoln Reserve and a multitude of others continued African Trench along Borderer and Beaucamp Ridges. Two hundred metres beneath the crest, Snap Trench connected African Trench and Snap Reserve with African Reserve. The garrisons of this maze of trenches were further assisted by the network of deep sunken lanes. In addition to the scores of recommissioned British dug outs and gun pits, the Germans had buried deep into the lanes' substantial banks to create improvised redoubts.

Followed by its Pioneer battalion, the 7/York & Lancs, the 17th Division had advanced up the Fins gap on 6 September. The Pioneers' chronicler recalled that there remained a great many partridges in the area which, despite the best efforts of the transport officer and his 12-bore shot gun, suffered 'no serious diminution in their numbers'.[1] On 9 September, Lancashire Fusiliers of the Northern Division made the first serious attempt to penetrate the defences south-west of Gouzeaucourt. Avoiding the gas-filled shell holes of Dessart Wood, the 10th Battalion moved up during a very dark night to positions south of the Metz-Gouzeaucourt road opposite Heather Support. It was an inauspicious start for in the murk platoons became intermingled, lost direction and a number of men succumbed to the effects of seeping blue cross gas. At 4am a 'good though rather too rapidly moving'[2] barrage came down, followed five minutes later by the German response. The Fusiliers fought their way into Heather Support and sections of one company penetrated as far as the final objective, Heather Trench. German counter-attacks bombed them out and another advance down the Fins road threatened to turn the flank of the company in Heather Support. The Fusiliers hung on grimly to the first objective, having sustained 90 casualties in the two attacking companies.

On the left of the 17th, the New Zealand Division was ordered to take African Support and Trench. Like the Fusiliers, the New Zealanders experienced difficulties as they formed up on the western edge of Gouzeaucourt Wood. When they commenced their advance, German machine-gun fire was fortunately high and erratic. The 2nd Rifles fought through the wood and then took Queen's Cross and African Support. Its left company and the 3rd Battalion were held up by fire from a strong point in Dead Man's Corner and from the garrison of Snap Reserve. Corporal Fruin and his section stormed the stronghold and bombed up 20 yards of African Support, only to be forced back by a determined counter-attack and a rapidly dwindling supply of bombs. The party was ejected from Dead Man's Corner but held on to African Support. Another attempt on Dead Man's Corner the following day again proved initially successful, but it was lost that same evening when Germans wearing captured British helmets surprised the defenders.

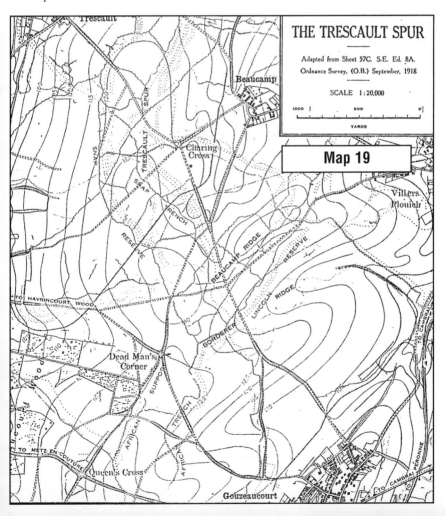

THE TRESCAULT SPUR

Adapted from Sheet 57C. S.E. Ed. 8A.
Ordnance Survey. (O.B.) September, 1918

SCALE 1:20,000

YARDS

Map 19

The next major effort against Gouzeaucourt and the ridges to its north-west was made by the 38th, New Zealand and 37th Divisions on 12 September. Of the three, the 38th Division was least involved, supplying one company to advance towards Heather Trench in order to cover the right flank of the New Zealanders. The latter were to go for Dead Man's Corner, Snap Reserve and Snap Trench, with a final objective of Charing Cross on the crest before Beaucamp. This position, which for most of 1917 had provided accommodation for command dugouts, was the boundary with 13/RB of 111 Brigade. With the RB on the right and 13/KRRC on the left, the 37th Division was ordered to take Trescault and Bilhem. Contemporary intelligence reports suggested that Bilhem had again been strongly fortified by the enemy.

At 5.25am on 12 September a creeping barrage of HE and machine-gun fire, supplemented by a hurricane bombardment of four medium and six light trench mortars directed on Dead Man's Corner, heralded the advance. Although the New Zealand right was hampered by the failure of the Welsh to get forward, the 2nd Rifles 'poured' into African Trench and commenced 'deadly execution'.[3] In the face of such determination the garrison of Dead Man's Corner succumbed. Sergeant Harry Laurent surged on a further 700 yards until he came up against the enemy support line west of Gouzeaucourt. With only seven men, Laurent charged the trench, killed 20 defenders and captured the remainder. His position was, however, untenable. Taking fire from all sides, Laurent shot a few 'fractious'[4] prisoners to calm the rest, and then withdrew his party, complemented by 111 prisoners and two dogs, to African Trench. He was subsequently awarded the VC.

In the centre and on the left, the 1st and 4th Battalions gained Snap Reserve but, on trying to get out and on, came under 'extraordinarily heavy'[5] machine-gun fire from Snap Trench and Beaucamp Ridge.

Looking across Scrub Valley to the northern edge of Gouzeaucourt Wood. The slope up which the New Zealanders struggled to attack Snap Reserve is clearly evident.

One small party of the 4th Battalion probably reached Charing Cross, but the bulk of the two units remained pinned down in Snap Reserve. In the evening the 4th Battalion made another attempt and reached Snap Trench, although its effort to get on to the Trescault-Gouzeaucourt road was frustrated. It consolidated on the ground gained, with its most advanced post some 100m west of Charing Cross.

North of the New Zealanders, 13/RB advanced north-east towards the crest of Trescault Spur. Under intense fire and despite several subsequent counter-attacks, the battalion reached and held its first objective. The 13/KRRC took Trescault village without too much difficulty but was halted by fire from a strong point on its right. Fortunately 13/RB witnessed the problem and sprayed Lewis-gun fire into the flank of the enemy position. The KRRC got on and, despite heavy casualties, by 7.30am had taken Bilhem and 190 prisoners. Enemy gas and high explosive continued to plaster the positions until the 10/RF came up to relieve them during the night. For the next three days the Fusiliers experienced an exceptionally uncomfortable time in posts and trenches straddling the Trescault-Ribécourt road and among the ruins of Bilhem. Assaulted by German bombers, low-flying aircraft and swept by machine-gun fire, the battalion resolutely hung on to the gains. If the next stage of the operation was to be successful, it was essential that the Fusiliers did remain where they were.

The New Zealand Division was also having a frenetic time a little to the south. On 13 September the 1st Auckland and 1st Wellington Battalions had tried to ease forward towards Gouzeaucourt and Borderer Ridge but strong German resistance repulsed them. In the early hours of 14 September German troops supported by liquid fire drove the New Zealanders back to African Support, where they held firm. The division had suffered heavy casualties during the preceding five days, yet the crests of Borderer and Beaucamp Ridges remained in German hands.

The 5th Division relieved the battered New Zealanders and in the drenching rain of 18 September sent two companies of the 2/KOSB against African Trench. As soon as the advance began, machine-gun fire ripped into the ranks, knocking out all the officers. The few men who succeeded in getting to the objective were immediately bombed out and then, as they withdrew to their start line, were caught in enfilade from the lane running between Caesar's Camp and Dead Man's Corner.

The real purpose of the KOSB effort was to protect the left flank of a much greater offensive to the south. The northern end of this assault

African Support

The eastern edge of Gouzeaucourt Wood with the trees of Dead Man's Corner centre. The track from Queen's Cross no longer reaches the clump at Dead Man's Corner. African Support ran almost parallel to the track 70m to its east.

involved an attack on African and Heather Trenches south of the Metz-Gouzeaucourt road by the 38th Division. The Welsh Division's right brigade, with (left to right) the 15/Welch, 14/Welch and 13/Welch, was to push over Heather Trench and reach a sunken lane running roughly mid-way between the Révelon-Gouzeaucourt road and the railway. The brigade passed through an uncomfortable blue cross barrage on its way to the start lines, but reached their objectives and began to consolidate. On the left of the brigade, the 13/Welch gained its final objective on the Fins road but discovered that 113 Brigade, north of the road on its left, was not up. With the exception of a handful of men, the 14/RWF and 16/RWF had remained pinned in their original trenches. With only four surviving company officers and having been reinforced by one platoon of the divisional Pioneers, the 13/Welch threw back its left to form a defensive flank to its original front line; this covered what was thought to be a gap of about 500m between it and the Fusiliers. With communications to its two sister battalions on the right and its own rear positions hampered by German snipers and machine-gun fire from Gouzeaucourt, the 13/Welch knew little of what was going on. Corps orders in fact intended the advance by 114 Brigade and the 17th Division to its south-east to continue and push north along the ridge east of Gouzeaucourt. The plan was to take Gauche Wood and Quentin Ridge, thereby encircling the village and pinching it out. As communications with the Welch Brigade were so poor, the responsibility devolved on the 17th Division. The 14/RWF made several attempts to push on but had to fall back on African Support where the 16/RWF were in touch with the 2/KOSB. Further efforts by

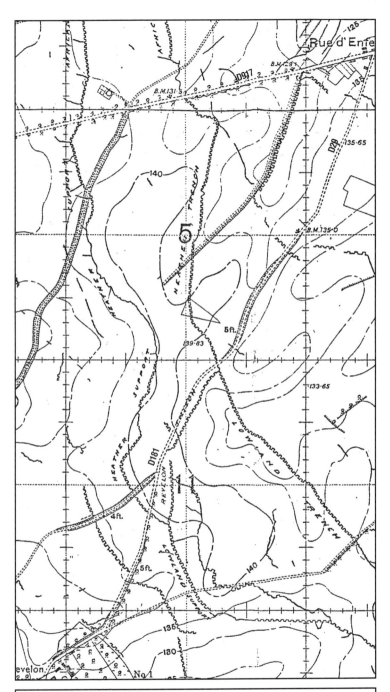

Map 20. SW of Gouzeaucourt: September 1918

With Dessart Wood in the distance this photograph shows the land traversed by African Support and Trench south of the Metz-Gouzeaucourt road (D29B) east of Gouzeaucourt Wood. In September 1918 the 38th Division attacked right to left.

113 Brigade on 19 September south of the Metz-Gouzeaucourt road did eventually bear fruit with the capture of African Trench.

It had been an exhausting, exasperating and costly two days for the Welsh Division. The four battalions of the Welch Regiment (including the Pioneers), had lost over 100 killed and nearly 500 wounded. Figures for 113 Brigade are more difficult to find, but on 18 September the 16/RWF alone had taken over 120 casualties, about one quarter of its strength.

A comparative lull of nine days then followed. Fighting did not cease in front of Beaucamp but it was restricted to patrols and artillery exchanges. Although it was appreciated by all concerned that, sooner rather than later, the ridges and the Hindenburg Line beyond would again have to be stormed, greater efforts were for the time being concentrated elsewhere.

The opportunity for IV Corps to recommence the offensive came on 27 September. The 42nd Division was to advance from Bilhem, with the Trescault-Ribécourt road on its left flank, cross Unseen Trench and Unseen Support south of Ribécourt and move on to Highland Ridge. The final goal was to capture the crest of Welsh Ridge but it was accepted that this could probably not be achieved on the first day. To the south of the East Lancashire Territorials, the 5th Division would go for Beaucamp and then wheel right to take Highland Ridge north of Villers-Plouich and Couillet Valley. Both divisions were to be supported by a total of 11 brigades of field artillery, four of heavy and ten trench-mortar batteries. To conform with advances to the north and the sweep of the line in IV Corps itself, zero hour for the different brigades was staggered. The 42nd Division, which imagined itself having to cross the lower slopes of Highland Ridge before Beaucamp on the high ground above had been taken by the 5th Division, complained about the decision but was told to get on with it.

The 5th Division knew it faced an exceptionally difficult task. On the left, the 1/Bedfordshire of 15 Brigade was to take Beaucamp, with one company of the 1/Cheshire acting as mopper-ups. The 16/Warwickshire was then to continue the advance onto Highland Ridge, in touch with the Lancashire Fusiliers of 125 Brigade on the left and 13 Brigade on the right. As cooperation between all units was vital, two battalions and the brigade TMB shared the same HQ dug out at the cross roads 600 yards north-east of Dead Man's Corner. With the intention of covering the gap between the 1/Bedfordshire and its own company which was to enter the village from the west, one company of the 1/Cheshire was detailed to fire a grazing barrage towards the south-west corner of Beaucamp.

On the right of the divisional front, 13 Brigade had a shorter distance to travel but was dependent upon 15 Brigade taking the village. The brigade was to advance through the gap between the village and Villers-Plouich, with the 14/Warwickshire on the left and the 1/West Kent on the right. Things went wrong from the start. An enemy bombardment knocked out most of 13 Brigade's heavy trench mortars and the British barrage was too light to keep the Germans sheltering in their dug outs. The West Kent had a battalion front of about 1000 yards and was already hugely under establishment. As soon as the troops appeared above the crest of Beaucamp Ridge, withering

A steel pill box, which housed a German anti-tank gun, under inspection by New Zealand troops.

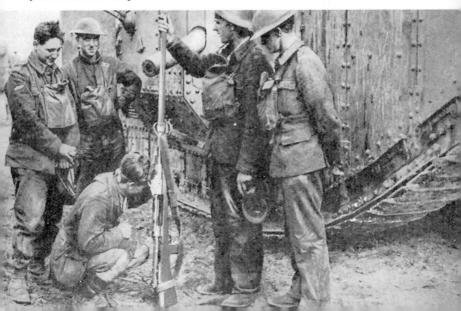

fire swept into the ranks; one strong point which caused particular trouble was housed in the wrecked hull of a British tank. The tanks allotted to the West Kent soon ditched and in the face of such adversity, the survivors dug in only some 200 yards from their start line. The 15/Warwickshire reached to within 300 yards of the Beaucamp-Villers-Plouich road but, having lost its tanks and with a casualty list of over 160, the battalion was forced to withdraw from its gains. The Bedfordshire had also made little permanent progress. The accompanying tanks were soon knocked out but Beaucamp was taken and mopped up. However, German counter-attacks drove a gap between the two brigades and forced both the Bedfords and the Cheshires from the ruins.

Two Lancashire Fusilier battalions of 125 Brigade attacked to the left of 15 Brigade. The tanks which were supposed to knock out the machine-gun nests in Beaucamp Valley and its slopes, quickly ditched and uncut wire further obstructed the Fusiliers. The 8th Battalion lost nine officers and 132 men in 30 minutes and members of one company of the 7th fell victim to the British barrage. A German counter-attack towards Lancaster Road brought a very faltering advance to a halt. The 5/Manchester of 127 Brigade led off from Trescault Ridge followed by the 7th and 6th Battalions. Four of the six tanks were knocked out or broke down almost immediately but the 5th reached the first objective and the two other battalions pressed on towards Plush Trench. On the right, the 7th Battalion suffered from an exposed flank; with the Fusiliers bogged down and the 5th Division not in control of Beaucamp, German machine-gunners concentrated on the Manchesters. By 11am A Company was down to 55 men and C to 32, with no officers. Lieutenant Gresty and a party of about 40 crossed Unseen Trench and Unseen Support, reached the Villers-Plouich-Ribécourt road at the bottom of the slope, captured two German field guns and then, with both flanks in the air, withdrew to Argyle Road. Touch was gained with the 6th Battalion on the left which had also crossed the Hindenburg Line, but neither battalion could do much more until Boar Copse was cleared by the Fusiliers. Even when this was achieved, the Manchester battalions were so few in number that they could not get on beyond the Villers-Plouich road. Ribécourt village had been entered at 10.30am by the 4/RF who, according to its chronicler, 'carried out a business-like advance'.[6] The Fusiliers handed over to the 5/KOYLI of the 62nd Division which pressed on towards Kaiser Trench.

When darkness fell on 27 September, neither the 42nd nor the 5th

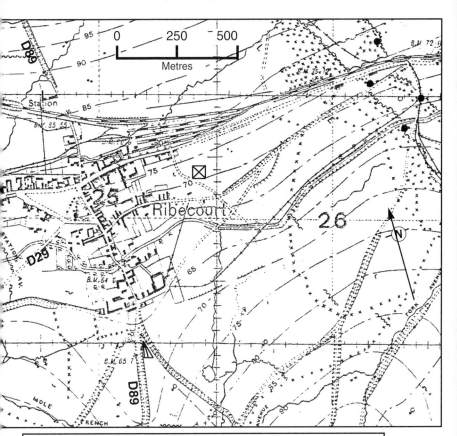

Map 21. Ribécourt: 20 September 1917

Divisions had achieved their objectives. The Manchesters had made most progress, but they and the Lancashire Fusiliers had been very roughly handled. True, over 350 German dead were later buried by the Manchester Brigade but of the 450 attackers of the 7th Battalion, only 150 remained. Orders to renew the offensive had already been drawn up and preparations were in train to ensure that in the early hours of 28 September the two divisions would enjoy better success.

The night of 27-28 September was very dark and punctuated by spells of heavy rain. On the 5th Division's front the staff had decided to bring forward 95 Brigade from Winchester Valley to pass through 15 Brigade opposite Beaucamp; 15 Brigade would then side-step to replace the weaker 13 Brigade. It was anticipated that if 95 Brigade could take Beaucamp and the southern section of Highland Ridge above Villers-Plouich, it would turn the flank of the enemy in front of 13 Brigade, forcing him to withdraw. The 42nd Division brought up the Oldham Territorials of the 10/Manchester to pass through the weakened 6th and 7th Battalions; their objective was to secure the previous day's objectives of Highland and Welsh Ridges. On their right the Lancashire Fusiliers would advance from their positions in Beaucamp Valley, cross Argyle Road and link up with 95 Brigade on the high ground above Villers-Plouich.

The darkness, weight of traffic in Trescault Valley and an enemy barrage delayed 95 Brigade on its way up to the front. Furthermore, at 2.35am the two attacking battalions were told that zero had been brought forward to 2.40am. Struggling against a tide of men and vehicles, and having lost one platoon on the way, the 1/Devonshire finally reached the start line at 2.30am. On its left the 1/East Surrey had experienced similar difficulties and had appreciated the 1/Cheshire's welcome assistance in getting them into position. The two leading companies of the Devonshire were immediately caught in enfilade and held up by wire in front of Beaucamp; both companies fell back to their start line and reorganised. Meanwhile the East Surrey had made more progress assisted, so their diarist believed, by the darkness rendering the German musketry ineffective. The Surrey drove the enemy from Snap Trench, forged into Beaucamp and cleared York Trench beyond. Encouraged by the success on their left, the Devonshire attacked again, occupied Lincoln Reserve and then bombed their way down Dunraven Trench towards Villers-Plouich. As their 13th Battalion had done 17 months before, the East Surrey cleared the village and reached Surrey Road on the western slopes of

The gentle slope of the Trescault Spur running down to Beaucamp Valley. The trees (centre left) are Boar Copse. Lancaster Road runs along the embankment (centre). In September 1918 Lancashire Fusiliers of the 42nd Division were caught in the open by German machine guns in Beaucamp (off right) as they tried to gain Highland Ridge.

Boar Copse   Lancaster Road   Highland Ridge   Couillet Wood

5th Manchester

7th and 8th Lancashire Fusiliers

Welsh Ridge. Under cover of massed Lewis gun fire the Devon dribbled men across the Gouzeaucourt road and gained touch with the Surrey near Village Road. In the evening the 1/Norfolk entered Flag Ravine and the 1/Cheshire occupied the profusion of dug outs in Fifteen Ravine; troops of the 1/DCLI and the 12/Gloucester passed through the jubilant East Surrey and Devonshire to form up for the advance towards La Vacquerie.

The 10/Manchester and the Lancashire Fusiliers had also been successful. Under a tremendous barrage the Oldhamers occupied the northern end of Highland Ridge, witnessing hordes of demoralised Germans streaming through Couillet Wood and up the slopes of Welsh Ridge. On their right the 7th and 8th Fusiliers crossed Argyle Road and linked with the East Surrey on Barrier Road. The Manchester and the the 5/LF pushed patrols through Couillet Wood, crossed the railway and, flushed with success, surged onto Welsh Ridge. A squadron of the 3/Hussars reached Good Man Farm and, despite their low numbers, the 8/LF and the 8/Manchester gained the labyrinth of trenches on the crest.

The 5th and 42nd Divisions had enjoyed a very successful day, at surprisingly little cost. In two days of fighting the 42nd had pierced the Hindenburg Line to a depth of 5000 yards for a total of just under 1100 casualties; in the 5th Division, the Devonshire, for example, had lost 43 and the East Surrey 25. The remarkably low casualty list was attributed to a number of factors. One writer believed it to be a combination of skilful use of the ground, excellent use of covering fire and a readiness by junior commanders to by-pass areas of resistance and exploit opportunities when they arose. Another factor was the sound coordination between different arms. Three supply tanks were allocated to the 5th Division and aircraft of 59 Squadron dropped small arms ammunition by parachute to forward troops. There was also a degree of international cooperation as a battery of New Zealand 6-inch Newtons provided devastating support for 15 Brigade. Finally, although the German machine-gunners fought with their expected valour and determination, there was an increasing propensity among the ordinary soldiery to surrender when faced by the bayonets of British infantry.

There was, however, little time for units of the 5th Division to spend in mutual congratulation. The 42nd was relieved by the New Zealand Division but the 5th remained in the line and received fresh orders to continue the advance. The 1/DCLI and the 12/Gloucester barely had time to assemble on Fusilier Ridge before the barrage signalled the opening of the next attack. Their objective was the Gonnelieu-La Vacquerie road beyond Cemetery Ridge; once that had been reached, 15 Brigade was to pass through, cross the Hindenburg Line and advance to Banteux. Unfortunately, the barrage moved far too quickly for the infantry who had to pick and stumble their way through the shell-tossed ruins of abandoned trenches and wire. Enemy machine guns sprayed them from the right and by the time the sunken road was reached, both brigades had become hopelessly mixed. The plan for the 1/Cheshire to capture Barrack Trench and Support and for the 1/Norfolk to pass through and continue on to Bleak Support and Bleak House was necessarily abandoned. The division was to make no further progress that day, but it was at least in touch with the New Zealanders near the south-west corner of La Vacquerie. Even Brigade sympathised with the difficulties faced by the troops:

> Taking into consideration the short notice given of the impending attack and the intermediate march east of two and three kilometres in the darkness to positions...and the fact that troops had barely reached these positions when they had to advance, and that in one case the attacking battalion had not been extended when the barrage fell on the enemy trenches...the strength, fortitude and gallantry with which these attacks were pressed home by the men, cannot be too highly commended.[7]

Such was the confusion of trenches on the crest of Welsh Ridge that there was no satisfactory forming-up line for the New Zealanders when they relieved the Lancashire Territorials. It was decided to withdraw the forward troops from the ridge 30 minutes before zero to enable the New Zealand barrage to come down 200 yards east of Surrey Road. The Kiwis had moved up through a heavy bombardment of Trescault Valley and Beaucamp, losing touch with two companies of 1 Brigade on the way. At 3.30am the battalions moved forward. The 1st Canterbury on the right passed over the crest of Welsh Ridge and, after some severe fighting, cleared the ruins of La Vacquerie. Losing direction among the tangled wire and tumbled trenches, the support companies passed to the south of the village and into the 5th Division's area. One party managed to reach the Cambrai road south-west of the village but, with the 5th Division held up on their right, withdrew to the village and gained touch with the Cornwall. Back on the ridge, the 2nd Otago retook Good Man Farm, fought its way through the Hindenburg system and dropped down into La Vacquerie Valley. On the extreme left, 1 Brigade crested Bonavis Ridge, reached Lateau Wood and saw on the eastern side of the canal, woods untouched by war and the towers and spires of Cambrai. Although the New Zealanders did not yet know it, to their south the 46th Division had stormed the St Quentin Canal near Bellenglise and American and Australian troops were approaching Bony and Bellicourt. As far as IV Corps was concerned, the fly in the ointment was the 5th Division's failure to get into the Hindenburg Line south of the Cambrai-Gouzeaucourt road.

Matters were rectified the following day. The 1/Cheshire and 1/Norfolk, which had both spent an uncomfortable night being trench-mortared and sniped in Flag Ravine and on Fusilier Ridge, struck south and east at 4am on 30 September. The two battalions broke through Barrack Trench and Support, pushing patrols along the Gonnelieu Ridge to the high ground above Banteux. Enemy troops and transport were seen crossing the canal but most escaped before the British artillery could be directed upon the inviting targets. In the opinion of the Cheshires' chronicler, 15 Brigade's successful advance was the result of the well directed barrage and of the 'liberties taken in various ways during the battles, such as assembling and advancing without reconnaissance'.[8]

The recapture of Welsh Ridge and La Vacquerie did not of course end the battle. The 37th Division, which had been resting since its time at Trescault, relieved the 5th on the night of 30 September and continued to pursue the Germans across the canal and on in the direction of Le Cateau. Trescault, Beaucamp, Villers-Plouich, Gouzeaucourt (which had been occupied almost without opposition by the 21st Division on 28 September) and the ridges again became rear areas. Squadrons of cavalry, brigades of artillery and the multifarious units which supply the requirements of an army swarmed over the slopes and sheltered in the valleys. In time the railway was relaid, the fields cleared of wire, the trenches filled in and the villages rebuilt. Besides the occasional concrete pill box or command post, within a few years all that would remind visitors of the tumult the area had witnessed were the cemeteries.

NOTES
1. M.Gilvary, *The History of the 7th Battalion York & Lancs*, p.83
2. J.Latter, *The History of the Lancashire Fusiliers*, p.386
3. H.Stewart, *The New Zealand Division, 1916-1919*, p.481
4. Ibid. p.482
5. Ibid. p.483
6. O'Neill, op.cit. p.313
7. E.Wyrall, *The History of the DCLI in the Great War*, p.415
8. A.Crookenden, *The History of the Cheshire Regiment*, p.161

CEMETERIES

Fifteen Ravine British Cemetery

Despite its name, the cemetery is actually in Farm Ravine. It was sometimes referred to as Farm Ravine Cemetery but later took its current name from the fifteen trees which originally lined the depression taken by the 12/SWB. It was begun by the 17/Welch to bury the dead of the 40th Division following its attack on Villers-Plouich and Fusilier Ridge. Most of these original burials lie in Plot I, row C. When it was lost to the Germans in March 1918 there were 107 graves. After the war a great deal of concentration took place and there are now 1,220 burials. More than three-fifths of the total are unknown.

The remains of Argyll & Sutherland Highlanders killed at Beaucamp were brought in from Argyle Road Cemetery. Over 170 others came from Bourlon German Cemetery and 79, largely RND, from a cemetery on the Marcoing road just beyond Villers-Plouich.

Dozens of regiments are represented, including those of scores of men from the 20th Division killed during the Cambrai operation. Among the rows of unidentified are many men of the 2nd, 11th and 14th DLI. There are also troops of the 42nd Division killed between April and June 1917 and in September 1918. Robert Pegram (I.B) of the 7/London, killed near Le Transloy in October 1916, was brought in during the post-armistice concentration. Second Lieutenants George Young and Alan Wylie MC of 15 Squadron are in VII.E. They were pilot and observer in an RE8 shot down by machine-gun fire on the opening day of the Battle of Cambrai. Another RE8 crew lie next to each other in V.C. Captain T.Symons DFC and Second Lieutenant F.Chadwick of 59 Squadron were brought down near Lateau Wood on 29 September 1918. Symons was formerly a member of the Royal Sussex and Chadwick, the Coldstream Guards.

Gouzeaucourt New British Cemetery

This large cemetery which now contains the remains of over 1200 British and Dominion servicemen, was begun in November 1917. The original burials are in Plot III. After the war there was a substantial degree of concentration. Many of the 38th Division of September 1918 were brought in from Arvon Cemetery near Heudicourt and 44 New Zealanders from a cemetery near Gouzeaucourt Wood. Other men killed during the recapture of the village and its surrounds came from Genin Well Copse Cemetery near Chapel Hill. Some 2/RB killed in April 1917 were concentrated from the quarry immediately east of the railway on the Villers-Guislain road. There are nearly 400 unidentified, many of whom are Welsh Guards killed on 1 December 1917.

Among the individuals are Lance-Sergeant Lambie, 14/A & SH, whose wife and two children were drowned on the Lusitania (VI.H), CSM Loveday, 1/Wiltshire, DCM and Bar (VIII.E), Second Lieutenant Frederick Bentley DCM, a rare example of a commissioned ranker serving in the Guards Division (III.A), and Lieutenant-Colonel Liston-Foulis of the Royal Marine Artillery (IV.A). Next to each other in V.A. are Lieutenant Rowland Coles and Second Lieutenant John Day of 52 Squadron. Their BE2e was shot down on 9 May 1917 by one of Germany's most successful aces, Leutnant Werner Voss of Jasta Boelke. Voss's usual mount was an Albatross Scout with a heart and laurel leaves painted on the fuselage; next to them he had another symbol, a swastika. Coles, from Taunton, had served on Gallipoli with the West Somerset Yeomanry. His brother had been killed there with the 4/East Lancashire Territorials in June 1915. A crew of another BE2e of 52 Squadron are in V.E. and VI.B. Captain Arthur Baker and Second Lieutenant A.Etches disappeared over the French sector on 11 April 1917. Baker, who had attended the Royal School of Mines and Trinity Hall, Cambridge, came back from Siberia to enlist. He was commissioned into the DCLI and transferred to the RFC in 1916. Following a spate of accidents which culminated with the death of the CO, the squadron had swopped its superior RE8s for another squadron's second rate BE2es.

Metz-en-Couture Communal Cemetery British Extension

The cemetery was begun in April 1917 by the 20th Division following its capture of the village. After concentration, it now contains 467 British and Dominion burials and 12 Germans. Thirty-five corpses, largely from the 47th and 58th London Divisions, were brought from a small cemetery west of the village. There are also Territorials of the 59th Division.

Among the 63rd Division men are Lieutenant Commanders Shaw-Stewart and Campbell and Commander Charles West, all of whom were killed on Welsh Ridge on 30 December 1917. Captain George Paton, VC, MC, 4/Grenadier Guards, killed near Gonnelieu on 1 December 1917, lies in II.E. Captain John Urquhart, 14/Argyll & Sutherland Highlanders (IV.A.19), died of wounds received during the battalion's costly and abortive attack on Beaucamp. Two airmen of 52 Squadron killed on 14 April 1917 lie next to each other in III.A. Captain Alfred Skinner, 4/South Lancashire and 27 Squadron (II.8) was originally buried by the Germans in the communal cemetery. Skinner's squadron of 'Martinsyde Elephants' was returning from a bombing raid on Havrincourt Wood on 31 August 1916 when it was jumped by Jasta 1. The squadron lost four aircraft in the ensuing engagement. Skinner became the sixth of Leutnant Gustav Leffers's nine kills.

Ribécourt British Cemetery

The cemetery was begun by the 6th Division following its capture of the village on 20 November. It was used until March 1918 and then again in September and October. It now contains 289 burials, largely of the 1st and 11th

Leicestershire, 9/Norfolk and 8/Bedfordshire. There are also a few cavalry and men from the RND and 61st Division. Eighty-one of the burials are commemorated by special memorials.

Second Lieutenant Hugh Amesbury had served with the 1st Canadian Division at Ypres and on the Somme, but was killed when fighting with the 8/Bedfordshire at Ribécourt on 20 November 1917. The 303rd Siege Battery RGA also used the cemetery to bury its dead. Corporal Fred Sharp failed to turn up for roll call on 22 November 1917. His body was eventually recovered from the depths of a partially hidden but uncovered well. Second Lieutenant Thomas Ainscough and BSM Steel, also of the 303rd, are in the same row as Sharp.

Ribécourt Railway Cemetery

A small, compact cemetery of 52 burials which was begun by the 3rd Division in October 1918. It contains a few gunners and men of the 13/King's, 1/Gordon Highlanders and 2/Suffolk. There are also two former RE, killed while serving with the 704th Labour Company. Sergeant Percy Dolman, MM and Bar of the 1/Gordon lies in B.5.

Ribécourt Road Cemetery

Originally known as Divisional Cemetery, the plot lies a little to the east of the 42nd Division's memorial. It was begun by the 51st Division in November 1917 but the greatest number are burials of the 42nd Division killed in September 1918. Most are Manchesters of 127 Brigade and Lancashire Fusiliers of 125 Brigade. Private George Heard, DCM, MM of the 1/7th LF lies in IV.B.1 The only man of the 10/Manchester is Second Lieutenant Tom Wilson. According to Henry Lawson in his book *Vignettes of the Western Front*, Wilson had a premonition of his death the night preceding the attack on Highland Ridge.

The compact Sunken Road Cemetery on the lane between Villers-Plouich and Beaucamp. The route of a long communication trench called Lincoln Avenue lay close to the cemetery.

Sunken Road Cemetery, Villers-Plouich

Almost on the route of the communication trench known as Lincoln Avenue, this small cemetery of 59 burials nestles on the lower slopes of Highland Ridge. They are mainly men of the RND killed in December 1917 and January 1918 but there are also a few from the 59th and 61st Divisions. Petty Officer Williamson, MM and Bar of the 189th TMB lies at the end of the row. Rifleman Fred Williams is in the middle of the plot. He has a London Rifle Brigade badge, number and inscription. The register has him belonging to the 5th Battalion, London Irish Rifles, but no such battalion ever existed. Williams had enlisted, trained and fought with the LRB and when its 2nd Battalion was disbanded, was posted to the Artists.

Trescault Communal Cemetery

This cemetery contains only seven British graves, four of which are of 12/RB and 12/KRRC killed when Trescault was captured in April 1917. Lieutenant Nathaniel Pearce, 4/Grenadier Guards, lies in isolation in the bottom right-hand corner.

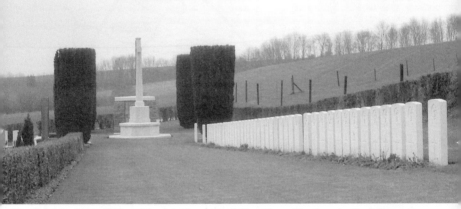

The British plot in Villers-Plouich Communal Cemetery. The lane to the left runs up to the site of the Monument on Surrey Road.

Villers-Plouich Communal Cemetery

A British prisoner of war and Captain Tom Rees of the RFC were buried back to back by the Germans in 1916. The main British plot was used between November 1917 and January 1918, mainly by the RND. Lieutenant John Edens of the Newfoundland Regiment died of wounds on 20 November. There are several men of the Nelson Battalion, including Able Seaman John Nelson. One of his officers, Lieutenant Purser, who was killed on the same day, was buried separately at the foot of the steps leading to the cross of sacrifice.

TOURS

Number 1: General tour by car

From Gouzeaucourt take the D29 past **Gouzeaucourt New British Cemetery.** Across Gouzeaucourt Valley to the left, Gauche Wood crests Quentin Ridge and the railway can be discerned as a line of trees beneath. A compact clump of trees on the crest further south marks Birdwood Copse; the poplars and white roof of Vaucellette Farm are immediately after the copse. The almost indefinable crest of Chapel Hill rises in front of Vaucellette Farm. The hill, farm and Gauche Wood

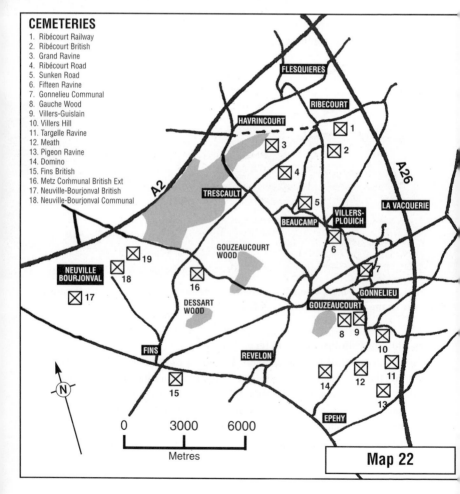

CEMETERIES
1. Ribécourt Railway
2. Ribécourt British
3. Grand Ravine
4. Ribécourt Road
5. Sunken Road
6. Fifteen Ravine
7. Gonnelieu Communal
8. Gauche Wood
9. Villers-Guislain
10. Villers Hill
11. Targelle Ravine
12. Meath
13. Pigeon Ravine
14. Domino
15. Fins British
16. Metz Communal British Ext
17. Neuville-Bourjonval British
18. Neuville-Bourjonval Communal

Map 22

A British pill box in Gouzeaucourt. In March 1918 its machine guns were intended to command Gouzeaucourt Valley and the western slopes of Quentin Ridge. Its garrison of the 9th Division resisted at least one German assault on 21 March but was withdrawn during the night when the village was evacuated.

were redoubts within the British Battle Zone of March 1918. To the right of the road lay Heather Trench and Support, while to the left, the continuation of these trenches were known as Lowland Trench and Support. Vincent's Force held positions along the road and on Révelon Ridge during the German counter-attack of November-December 1917.

Pass Révelon Farm and continue down to the D58 at Heudicourt. Turn right, pass **Fins New British Cemetery** and take the D917 towards Gouzeaucourt.

As you approach Gouzeaucourt, there are good views of Dessart Wood and later Gouzeaucourt Wood, both on the left. The site of the mill eventually taken by 2/RB in April 1917 is now a rough patch of ground 20m left of the road on the final crest before the road drops down into Gouzeaucourt village. African Support and Trench stretched away from the road across the fields to pass east of Gouzeaucourt Wood.

At the northern end of Gouzeaucourt, take the Villers-Plouich road (D56). A line of trees on the other side of the railway (and at 90 degrees to it) on the right marks Flag Ravine. In the valley bottom a track crosses the D56. The track to the left follows Fifteen Ravine while to the right it crosses the railway and climbs up onto Fusilier Ridge. In Villers-Plouich take the sign to **Sunken Road Cemetery** and climb up to Beaucamp. In the village the Chemin de Ribécourt (Argyle Road) is passable by car. Follow this down to **Ribécourt British Cemetery**. A single German bunker lies on the right side of the No Through Road immediately after the Mairie. A larger collection of them can be found either side of the D29, 1000m east of the village. These bunkers formed part of the Kaiser Trench and Kaiser Support system (Hindenburg Support Line). The slope of Highland Ridge climbs southward towards Couillet Wood.

Take the D89 back up the hill to Villers-Plouich. The remains of two German bunkers which formed part of Valley Trench (Hindenburg Main Line) are on the rough ground on the right (west) side of the road north of the pumping station. **Villers-Plouich Communal Cemetery** is on the D56 towards Marcoing.

At the southern end of Villers-Plouich follow the CWGC sign to the left towards **Fifteen Ravine British Cemetery**. Cross the railway and turn sharp right. (Straight on takes you onto Welsh Road but this is not passable by car.) Opposite the track down to the cemetery, the southern end of Surrey Road joins the tarmac near another pumping station. Stay on the main road and bear left towards La Vacquerie. This was Village Road. After a tour of the village, take the minor road which cuts across to the motorway slip road and the D917. Turn right and head towards Gouzeaucourt. Sonnet Farm now lies beneath the interchange but the Barracks is the house and rather dilapidated farm buildings a little further down on the left.

The 42nd Division's memorial on the Trescault-Ribécourt road (D17) commemorates the division's battles in Egypt, Gallipoli and the Western Front. The memorial faces the copse which now marks the site of Bilhem Farm.

Immediately after the Barracks, fork left to Gonnelieu. This was La Vacquerie Road. In the village, turn left onto the D96 towards Banteux. Bleak Trench became Quarry Trench just as a track joins the main road from the south 800m east of the village. This position shows the excellent observation enjoyed by the German outpost line over the British positions around Villers-Guislain. Do a U-turn and drive back into Gonnelieu.

Rejoin the D917 beyond the communal cemetery but cross straight over onto the D89 towards Villers-Plouich. This crosses Fusilier Ridge. The British front trenches between May 1917 and March 1918 were just to the right of the road. At the bottom of the slope Farm Ravine comes in from the left and **Fifteen Ravine Cemetery** can again be seen. In Villers-Plouich turn left and head back towards Gouzeaucourt.

As you approach the northern end of Gouzeaucourt, turn right onto the D29 to Trescault. This road climbs Borderer and Beaucamp Ridges, passes Charing Cross (where a minor road from Beaucamp joins) and crosses Trescault Spur. In Trescault turn right to **Ribécourt Road Cemetery**. On the left just beyond the village is the **42nd Division's** memorial. Opposite the memorial a track follows the trees which now mark the site of Bilhem. Go down this track beyond the dog-leg to appreciate how the German positions here commanded Beaucamp Valley and the exits from Beaucamp.

Return to the D17, drive back through Trescault and down to Metz. In Metz, turn left onto the D7. This road crosses Winchester Valley (left), passes **Metz Communal Cemetery Extension**, crosses Scrub Valley and bisects Gouzeaucourt Wood and Queen's Cross. A short diversion left at the cross roads of Queen's Cross gives good views across to the short line of trees which marks Caesar's Camp (east) and the small clump of trees in the field to the north-east which was Dead Man's Corner. Return to the D7 and turn left. African Support and Trench crossed the road about 800m and 1000m respectively, east of the wood.

Number 2: Metz and Beaucamp Ridge

Park at Metz and walk along the road towards Trescault (D17) for 600m until you come to a shrine on the right. Turn right and follow this lane down to a cross tracks. The railway siding, which carried, among other things, a naval gun during the Battle of Cambrai, followed the bottom of Winchester Valley. Turn left at the cross tracks and 400m after a deep quarry turn right onto a track which climbs up between banks and a line of trees. The quarry, now a dump, housed HQ dug outs, as did the banking on the side of the lane. The track meets another on Trescault Spur. Turn left and follow it, enjoying the views across Trescault Valley and Havrincourt Wood, to the Trescault-Gouzeaucourt road (D29). This is the area of Snap Trench and Reserve which caused so many problems to the New Zealanders in September 1918.

Turn right and walk along the road, passing to the west of Beaucamp, past Charing Cross, down the dip and up to the crest of Beaucamp Ridge. Here tracks come in from both left and right. The fields to the left in front of Beaucamp were those in which the 14/A & SH suffered so badly in April 1917 and which two brigades of the 5th Division attempted to cross in September 1918. Take the track to the right. In the fields to the left a clump of three small trees marks the site of Dead Man's Corner. This former strongpoint can only be reached by a track which runs through Caesar's Camp. The few trees cover what remains a substantial depression but there are no remains of any of the dug outs which once undermined its banks. The track curls to the right and drops down to a cross tracks in Scrub Valley. Turn left to follow the western edge of Gouzeaucourt Wood. This valley was full of gun batteries, aid posts, assembly trenches and shelters.

At the D7, turn right and climb up Dessart Ridge towards **Metz Communal Cemetery Extension**. On the bend before the cemetery, turn right onto a track. Metz mill used to stand here but walk 400m down the track to gain excellent views of the approaches across to Beaucamp Ridge and village. Return via the cemetery to Metz.

Number 3a: La Vacquerie and Welsh Ridge

Park at La Vacquerie and head north-east down the sunken lane which used to lead to Marcoing, (Rue Arnoult Tiroux de Grevillers). The lane itself becomes truly sunken and impassable but the track bears right onto the edge of a field. Just beyond the crest, cross the position of the Hindenburg Line and turn left at another track when you come to the trees surrounding the car park of the motorway rest area. Continue up this track which climbs Welsh Ridge between the Hindenburg Main and Support Line. On the left, just after the edge of a small wood which contains a few lumps of mouldering concrete, a small clump of four trees 100m into the field covers the remains of another German bunker. Just beyond the crest, turn left onto a track which passes the ruin of Good Man Farm. This is the area where Shepherd and Wain won their VCs. At the T-junction turn right. There

The entrance of a German bunker in the fields 1300m north-east of La Vacquerie. The bunker lay on the Hindenburg Main Line.

Good Man Farm was rebuilt on its original site after the war but is once again in ruins. A byre adjoins the living accommodation and, although dangerous to enter, the cellars which housed various British and German headquarters remain.

are good views across to the British positions at the Monument, Mountain Ash Trench and the German-held Couillet Wood

Drop down to another T-junction and turn right. This is Surrey Road. It is no longer possible to get along it to the site of the Monument, so follow it around to the main road (D56) and turn left towards Villers-Plouich. The British front line crossed the road where the stream is culverted beneath it. Visit the **communal cemetery** Continue up the small road which climbs above the cemetery to visit the site of the Monument. The ravine on the left was the strong point taken by Captain Crocker and the 13/East Surrey. It was on the approaches to the ravine that Corporal Foster won his VC. Return to the main road. Walk through the village in the direction of Gouzeaucourt and turn left towards **Fifteen Ravine Cemetery**. After visiting the cemetery climb the track by the pumping station opposite where the cemetery's access track joins the D89. Turn right at a T-junction. This is Welsh Road. Follow it across to La Vacquerie, passing through the position of Corner Work (top of a bunker visible in the field to the right) and back to the car.

Number 3b: Welsh Ridge and Vacquerie Valley

If time is not a problem, this longish walk covers much of the ground in this sector heavily contested during the Battle of Cambrai.

Park at La Vacquerie and take the right junction where the sunken lane to Marcoing goes straight on. This crosses the motorway (and the

Taken from Welsh Ridge looking south towards La Vacquerie. The white cottage (centre left) squats almost on the site of Corner Work. Corner Trench and Corner Support were a few metres to the right. The cottage fronts Welsh Road.

position of the Hindenburg Main Line) by a small bridge. Bear left after 200m. Straight ahead you can see Pam Pam Farm and Lateau Wood; to your right are the mast and trees surrounding Bleak House. Follow the tarmac, which soon becomes gravel, and descend. It curls round a small copse which lay just behind the Hindenburg Support Line. The track now becomes a grass path but, as it begins to descend towards Marcoing, again becomes gravel. A German light railway followed the route of the valley bottom and joined the track you are walking down near a large green gate. Continue until you reach a tarmac road with a calvary and turn right.

This small road runs south of the canal, roughly between Masnières and Marcoing. After 1100m turn right onto a gravel track and climb up the eastern slope of Welsh Ridge. At a T-junction, a left would take you back to Vacquerie Valley, but turn right and then left after 500m at another T-junction. This crosses the motorway by another small farm bridge and is the area where the 61st and 63rd Divisions were heavily engaged in December 1917. Ostrich Trench now lies beneath the motorway. Continue along the track, with Couillet Wood on Highland Ridge in front, almost until you reach the D56. Just before the tarmac, turn left and follow this grass track, which is the eastern end of Surrey Road until you reach a T-junction. Turn left. This lane has been recently widened to accommodate larger combine harvesters. Turn right almost at the crest to the position of the Hindenburg Line and pass Good Man Farm. At a junction 200m on, turn left and follow the well-defined track back to the sunken lane running to Marcoing. Turn right and return to La Vacquerie.

154

Number 4: Ribécourt and Highland Ridge

Park at Ribécourt Mairie. Walk down to cross *le Riot* on the Villers-Plouich road (D89) and visit **Ribécourt British Cemetery**. Take the tarmac lane behind the cemetery and climb up to the summit of Highland Ridge for excellent views in all directions. At the crest there is a cross tracks. Straight over would take you along the southern edge of Couillet Wood and down to the railway; right eventually drops down to Villers-Plouich but the path is not always passable. Turn left and descend until a junction 50m above a barn and five trees. Turn right and continue to descend to the German bunkers either side of the Ribécourt-Marcoing road. Walk back along the minor road to the south of the main one. This comes out at **Ribécourt Railway Cemetery**. A German bunker which held up the advance of the 51st Division on 20 November 1917 is on the right of the No Through Road, 300m west of the *Mairie*.

German bunker on Kaiser Trench a few metres south of the Ribécourt-Marcoing road. The tower of Ribécourt church can be seen in the distance.

The garrison of this German bunker on the western edge of Ribécourt enjoyed an excellent field of fire over troops of the 51st Division advancing towards the Flesquières Ridge on 20 November 1917.

Bibliography

C.Atkinson, *The Queen's Own Royal West Kent*, (London, 1929)

C.Atkinson, *The History of the Devonshire Regiment*, (London, 1928)

A.Atteridge, *History of the 17th (Northern) Division*, (Glasgow, 1929)

A.Barnes, *The Story of the 2/5th Gloucester Regiment*, (Gloucester, 1930)

R.Bond, *The King's Own Yorkshire Light Infantry in the Great War*, (London, 1929)

J.Boraston & C.Bax, *The Eighth Division in War*, 1914-1918, (Medici, 1926)

J.Burrows, *Essex Units in the War 1914-1919*

A.Crookenden, *History of the Cheshire Regiment in the Great War*, (Evans, 1938)

J.Ewing, *The History of the 9th (Scottish) Division 1914-1919*, (Murray, 1921)

C.Falls, *The Life of a Regiment. The History of the Gordon Highlanders*, (Aberdeen)

N.Franks, R.Guest & F.Bailey, *Bloody April, Black September*, (Grub Street, 1995)

F.Gibbon, *The 42nd (East Lancashire) Division 1914-1918*, (Country Life, 1920)

S.Gillon, *The KOSB in the Great War*, (Nelson & Sons)

M.Gilvary, *The History of the 7th (S) Battalion, the York & Lancs*, (Talbot, 1925)

T.Henshaw, *The Sky Their Battlefield*, (Grub Street, 1995)

A.Hussey & D.Inman, *The Fifth Division in the Great War*, (Nisbet, 1921)

V.Inglefield, *History of the 20th (Light) Division*, (Nisbet, 1921)

D.Jerrold, *The Royal Naval Division*, (Hutchinson, 1923)

J.Latter, *The History of the Lancashire Fusiliers*, (Gale & Polden, 1944)

T.Marden, *History of the Welch Regiment*, (1931)

T.Marden, *A Short History of the 6th Division*, (Rees, 1920)

A.Maude, *The 47th (London) Division*, (London, 1922)

F.Maurice, *The 16th Foot (Bedfordshire & Hertfordshire Regiment)*, (London, 1931)

W.Miles, *The Durham Forces in the Field*, (Cassell, 1920)

R.Moody, *The Historical Records of the Buffs*, (Medici, 1922)

S.Murphy, *The History of the Suffolk Regiment*, (Hutchinson, 1928)

J.Munby, *History of the 38th (Welsh) Division*, (Rees, 1920)

P.Oldham, *The Hindenburg Line*, (Leo Cooper, 1997)

H.O'Niell, *The Royal Fusiliers in the Great War*, (London, 1922)

H.Pearse & H.Sloman, *History of the East Surrey Regiment*, (London, 1924)

F.Petre, *The Royal Berkshire Regiment*, Vol.2

F.Petre, *The History of the Norfolk Regiment*, (Jarrold, n.d.)

A.Scott & P.Brumwell, *The History of the 12th Division*, (Nisbet, 1923)

L.Sellers, *The Hood Battalion*, (Leo Cooper, 1995)

W.Seymour, *The History of the Rifle Brigade in the War of 1914-1918*, (London, 1936)

A.Smithers, *The First Great Tank Battle*, (Leo Cooper, 1992)

H.Stacke, *The Worcester Regiment in the Great War*, (Cheshire & Sons, 1929)

H.Stewart, *The New Zealand Division 1916-1919*, (Whitcombe & Tombs, 1921)

H.Story, *The History of the Cameronians (Scottish Rifles) 1910-1933*, (Watson)

R.Woollcombe, *The First Tank Battle*, (Barker, 1967)

F.Whitton, *The History of the 40th Division*, (Gale & Polden, 1926)

W.Wood, *The History of the KSLI in the Great War*, (Medici, 1925)

H.Wylly, *The 1st and 2nd Battalions of the Leicester Regiment*,

H.Wylly, *The 1st & 2nd Battalions The Sherwood Foresters*, (Gale & Polden, n.d.)

E.Wyrall, *The Gloucester Regiment in the War*, (Methuen, 1931)

E.Wyrall, *The History of the Second Division 1914-1918*, (Nelson, 1922)

E.Wyrall, *The Duke of Cornwall's Light Infantry 1914-1919*, (Methuen, n.d.)

E.Wyrall, *The Somerset Light Infantry 1914-1919*, (Methuen, 1927)

The Official History of the Great War, France and Belgium. Various authors, (HMSO)

The Marquess of Anglesey, *A History of the British Cavalry 1816-1919,* (Leo Cooper, 1997)

Scrap Book of the 7th Battalion Somerset Light Infantry. No author, (Kingsbury 1931)

The History of the Prince of Wales Own Civil Service Rifles. No author. (Wyman, 1921)

The KRRC Chronicles

The Annals of the KRRC

SELECTIVE INDEX